# TIGER KING

# TIGER KING

## THE OFFICIAL TELL-ALL MEMOIR

# JOE EXOTIC

**GALLERY BOOKS**

NEW YORK   LONDON   TORONTO   SYDNEY   NEW DELHI

Gallery Books
An Imprint of Simon & Schuster, Inc.
1230 Avenue of the Americas
New York, NY 10020

Note: Some names have been changed.

First Gallery Books trade paperback edition November 2023

GALLERY BOOKS and colophon are registered trademarks
of Simon & Schuster, Inc.

For information about special discounts for bulk purchases,
please contact Simon & Schuster Special Sales at 1-866-506-1949
or business@simonandschuster.com.

The Simon & Schuster Speakers Bureau can bring authors
to your live event. For more information or to book an event,
contact the Simon & Schuster Speakers Bureau at 1-866-248-3049
or visit our website at www.simonspeakers.com.

Interior design by Michelle Marchese

Printed and bound by CPI Group (UK) Ltd, Croydon CR0 4YY

10  9  8  7  6  5  4  3  2  1

Library of Congress Cataloging-in-Publication Data is available
for the hardcover.

ISBN 978-1-9821-8042-3
ISBN 978-1-9821-8043-0 (pbk)
ISBN 978-1-9821-8044-7 (ebook)

*To Those I've Lost:*
*Mom, Dad, GW, Brian, Travis*

# PREFACE

Dear American Public,

Can you believe that bitch Carole Baskin is out there free as a bird while I'm sitting here rotting away in prison?

So much has changed since *Tiger King* came out on Netflix in 2020, but for me personally, so much has stayed the same. Nowadays everyone here calls me Tiger King. A lot of inmates who just came in the last year have watched it. The ones that haven't, their families all ask if they have met the Tiger King.

Did you notice how many people in *Tiger King* had no teeth, or very little? I saw this one meme that was mailed to me, where someone put a photo of a meat grinder with a man's legs sticking out on top, and next to it said "Carole's meat grinder," and on the bottom was a photo of my ex-husband John Finlay with his three teeth, and it said "Joe's meat grinder." That was the funniest shit I ever saw. In eleven years of being with John Finlay, I never saw him brush his teeth once.

The *Tiger King* documentary started filming nearly two years prior to my arrest. I knew a bunch of people in the industry were being interviewed, like my good friend Doc Antle, and I knew it was going to be an animal rights film, but I tried to use it as an opportunity to show the hypocrisy of these animal rights groups. What's the difference between my place and a place like Carole's Big Cat Rescue? We were both open to the public, we both took in big cats, we were nonprofit, we raised money. The only difference is I bred and she claims she don't.

I haven't seen the show and really don't care to because I know it's just gonna piss me off when I hear everyone lying about me. Right now I feel like the most famous homeless person there is. *Tiger King* done nothing to help me in here; in fact, it's made my life worse. The staff gets tired of sorting all the mail I get, and—to keep me from speaking with any media—they kept me in isolation for so long I damn near lost my mind.

People have suggested that I was addicted to fame. That's not true—it was never about fame. Work was my addiction. I wanted to become someone before I died. I did become someone, but I have yet to see what all the hype is about. I guess if I die tomorrow, I will have left my mark on this world, but I almost would rather not be associated with *Tiger King* now. It's turned into nothing but a shit show: people making things up to get their fifteen minutes of fame at my expense. How fast people forget you when you're out of sight, out of mind.

When I first became known as the Tiger King, I did it to help animals, and the people who love them. I raised money, I did Tigers for Tots at Christmas for kids in the hospital (which was a toy drive with bikers), I sent sick people on trips for their last wish, I rebuilt zoos that were in trouble. If someone had an animal they couldn't take care of, I wanted to help. If the government was trying to take someone's animal, I wanted to help. I fought for the rights of people to own animals and to stop laws that ban the private ownership of exotic animals.

Ever since I opened the Garold Wayne Exotic Animal Memorial Park, I have fought back against federal agencies impinging on my rights as an American citizen. That is what I stood up against for so long, until they convicted me of a felony and locked me up. I tell you what, I've seen some fucked-up shit in my life. I always knew firsthand that this country was full of corruption, and evil people preying on the innocent. I didn't know the half of it.

As far as I'm concerned, the government kidnapped me on trumped-up charges. They had two flimsy murder-for-hire charges against me that they knew wouldn't stick unless they made me out to be an animal-abusing monster. And the sad thing is, my story ain't even the worst of them. There are kids in this jail who made one mistake; now they're scarred for life because of this place. The prison industrial complex is a moneymaking machine, and very little of it gets spent on prisoners. It's modern-day slavery.

Everything you see on CNN right now is about systemic racism, and it's all bullshit and distraction. While people are knocking over two-hundred-year-old statues and rioting in the streets in the name of social justice, our government is kidnapping Black people and Mexicans by the thousands, forcing them into federal court, blackmailing them, and extorting them to sign plea deals. All to keep these prisons full. You put a breadwinner in prison, now the rest of the family goes on welfare, so taxpayers are paying every day for that breadwinner to be sitting in prison, working for next to nothing for a company called UNICOR.

The standards for what human prisoners are living in are far, far below the legal standards required for a chimpanzee in a zoo. Our government leaders should be ashamed of themselves. I don't think you're ever going to find an honest news media source willing to expose the politicians who are financially profiting from this. Thing is, when federal agents and prosecutors and judges steamrolled me the way I believe they did, they thought that would be the end of it. None of them expected the documentary on Netflix to become one of the most-watched television shows of all time. And while the US government can restrict my calls, restrict my access to my lawyers, keep me from sharing my story with the news media, they weren't able to keep me from writing this book.

I'm far from the only person the government has done this to, and there are many men in here who got a rawer deal than I did. The only reason my story matters more than anyone else's is because I'm the Tiger King. People often ask how I learned to work with big cats, and my answer is always the same: God taught me. It was like a superpower—a gift from God—to walk in a cage with twenty full-grown tigers and become one of them.

You think Carole ever gets in a cage with her tigers? I don't think so. Carole would be eaten alive by a grown tiger if she walked into its cage at Big Cat Rescue, because tigers can see your soul. She knows her tigers would eat her up, but rather than admitting it's a personal problem because her soul is so ugly, she tries to restrict people with good souls from interacting with animals. Her tigers don't have the kind of human interactions my cats had; they just sit in what looked to me like small, rusty cages all day while she makes money off them. The shame of it is, all my tigers are now her tigers. They aren't better off without me, I can promise you that.

People think I was obsessed with Carole, but in my mind it's the other way around: Carole was obsessed with me. She was paying thousands of dollars to have people follow me around. I filed complaints; they were all ignored. I was fighting for my life, and the only defense I could think of was to make clear I was a crazy son of a bitch you didn't want to mess with. Most exotic animal owners are obsessive, like a tick on a hound dog's ass. The only time they fall off is when they are done sucking the blood out of you, and they make sure the wound they left behind never heals. Some people get into the industry because they must dominate something in order to feel less helpless inside. Makes them feel powerful to be able to control a beast.

My bond with the animals was unexpected. It was never a choice to do what I did, I just stumbled upon this superpower. Carole Baskin was envious of my ability to work with tigers, and that's why she came after me for so many years.

This is the first time I've really gotten a chance to tell my side of the story. You might disagree with what I say, or think I'm a crazy ranting bastard, or maybe you won't think that much of it because you just see me as an entertaining guilty pleasure. That's your prerogative, but this is my perspective and I hope you'll come to understand me better.

It's a complicated story, but that's okay because I've got nothing but time to tell it. I've done my best to make it all make sense, so you can really understand what happened to me and who did what. With that said, there's no way I can tell everything. Hell, if I were to put every asshole who's ever done me wrong in this book, it would be as big as the White Pages and just as useless. So all you fuckers who bought this book just to see what I say about you, thank you for your money and I hope you enjoy the read. For everyone else, I promise I'll tell you everything you need to know so you'll appreciate who I am and what I stand for.

Maybe you think none of this has anything to do with you. Maybe you don't ever plan to own an exotic animal and don't understand why anyone would. Well, let me tell you, this ain't just about our government telling us what to do with exotics—it's just as bad with dogs. What would you do if someone tried to take your dog away? Whatever it takes to keep him, I bet. If you have a pit bull you love, I hope you hug him extra tight tonight because who knows if the government will allow you to hug that dog tomorrow.

Did you know in the dog-rescue world there is a thing called retail rescue? Yes, the animal rights people have shut down so many of the puppy mills and dog breeders, and worked to get the laws changed to ban selling puppies in pet stores so people have to go to privately run "nonprofit" organizations to adopt a dog or a puppy. Well, there is a shortage of puppies to sell in shelters, so they apparently fly in loads of them from places like France and auction them off to the very organizations that banned the breeding and sale of puppies to begin with. I imagine they lie and say they were rescued from other countries, but this is called "retail rescue," and seems to me it is done with the intention of creating a monopoly on adopting dogs. Money talks to people who are elected, and if you donate to the right people, you can get away with just about anything in this country.

If I die before I make it out of here, I want people to know I fought my ass off to help others. I want people to know what really happened at the zoo. I want people to know that no matter how hard life gets, you stand up and fight. If you have to look them right in the face and tell it like it is to get them to listen, then so be it. Don't apologize for shit if you know what's right.

I know I've made mistakes. And I have lived the hand I was dealt in life to the best of my ability, even in prison. I am the Tiger King. I will always be the Tiger King. No one can take that away from me.

I love you all,
Joseph Maldonado-Passage, a.k.a. Joe Exotic, a.k.a. the Tiger King
Federal Medical Center, Fort Worth Prison, August 2021

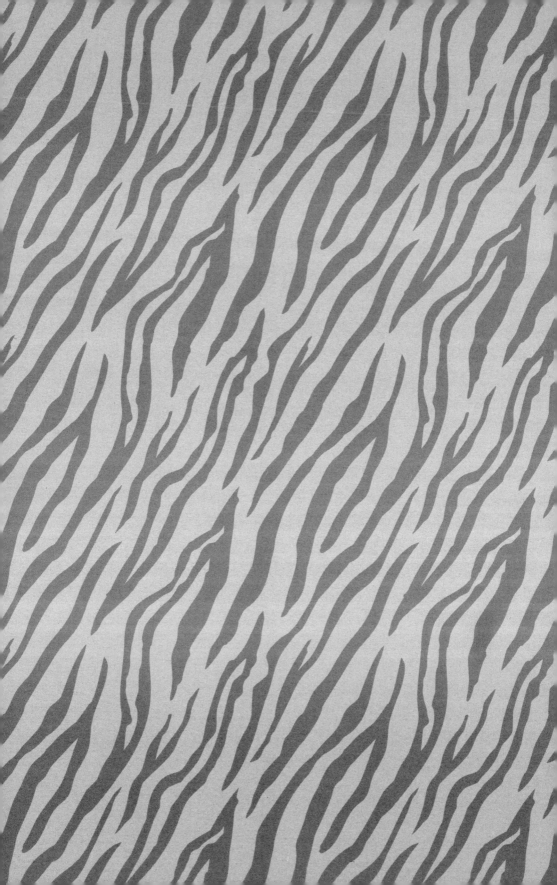

# PART ONE

# THE ORIGIN OF A SUPERHERO

# CHAPTER 1

The youngest I can remember, I was already a cowboy.

There was no age requirement to hack weeds out of the milo fields with a machete; that was something we all had to do. It was considered a neighborhood curse if there were weeds in your cornfield, so all the kids had to walk the fields pulling weeds out of crops. I had a brother and a sister that were much older than me, Yarri and Tammy, and a baby sister, Pamela. And then there was Garold Wayne, also known as GW. He was three years older than me, and he was my best friend.

We lived south of Garden City, Kansas, on a cattle farm in a community called Plymell. Our farm had large herds of cattle on wheat fields, fenced in with a hot wire. When it stormed, and wet or frozen tumbleweeds grounded the electric fence, GW and I would walk around and pull them off so the electric circuit would continue. All of us worked on the farm, including my father and mother. Neither of my parents did much else other than work.

Across a two-lane road from our house and farm were three

labor houses, where Hispanic workers lived during the harvest season. They would come help with the sugar beets and chop weeds from the fields with a Rogan knife so they didn't smother good crops out. During corn, milo, and wheat harvest, us kids would stand out on the main highway with signs that said we were hiring combines to harvest the crops.

When I was five, Dad decided I was old enough to start driving. That sounded good to me; it was basically a promotion. Dad would put a pickup in gear, with a hammer on the gas pedal, and I'd steer the truck while Yarri and GW loaded irrigation pipe on the trailer. I kept falling asleep in the seat, so that promotion didn't last long.

One day in the field, we were using an irrigation ditch to water the corn and Yarri done something wrong, causing the ditch to wash out. Dad was so mad, he held Yarri under the ditch water for a long time, nearly drowning him. My father was a mean man. Anytime we did something wrong Dad took it out on us. If Dad ever did something wrong he took it out on us too, with whatever was in reach.

At the house we had a feedlot, for those to be fattened up for slaughter sales. They ate a special mix called silage, which was ground-up corn stalks with the ears of corn in it. When silage got all packed together you could see steam come off it—that is how hot it got—and over time the corn became sour and had a really pleasant but deadly smell to it. One of our neighbors was inside one of the corn bins one day and the fumes from the fermenting corn overpowered him and killed him.

There was also a rodeo arena right there on the farm, and on Sundays we would have a community rodeo after church. The nuns would cook and serve food, and all the neighbors would rope, ride bulls, and barrel race. So between that and the feedlot, GW and I spent most our lives with animals.

It's crazy what I can and can't remember from my childhood. I often say I have a photographic memory, and I do indeed remember so much about working on the farm, but I can't really picture what Mom and Dad looked like back then. It's like their faces have been erased from my memory.

Dad was a thin man. The only clothes he had were work clothes because he was always working, either in the fields or with the cattle and horses. We were born to work the farm for him as free labor, just as he and his twelve brothers and sisters all worked in the fields. It was tradition. He had us kids drinking hard liquor at very young ages, which was apparently a German tradition.

Mom . . . when I picture Mom at her youngest, I see a thin lady with a beehive hairdo. But I can't remember much else. Mom was a good cook; made a lot of German dishes. She was always canning things like pickles, okra, and peaches and stuff. When Dad was not around she took us to the fields and worked just as hard as anyone did. One time she got kicked in the back by one of Dad's horses. It gave her problems her whole life, but it never stopped her from working.

Mom tried to make time for us to be kids, watching cartoons and eating breakfast before all the chores started. We never listened to music much, just some German stuff my dad liked. None of us watched much television, but Mom and Dad both liked westerns like *Bonanza*, and GW and I would watch Mom watch her stories, *Days of Our Lives* and *As the World Turns*.

There weren't many times we ever went to town, other than to go to the dentist, the doctor, or to Mom's hair parlor. We'd go to the drive-in movies once in a while and Dad would make us lie down in the back under blankets so we could get in for free. My parents never talked about money and hardly ever spent any. Throughout my childhood and even into adulthood, I never saw my parents buy new clothes; they shopped at garage sales and bought everything on sale. Mom would give her last dime to someone else before she spent it on herself. She wore the same blue coat for twenty years.

My favorite memory of my mother is from when I was ten years old. I remember it like it was yesterday. There was a light summer rain, and Mom and I were out in the wheat field, alone, pulling a calf from a young cow that could not give birth on her own. To help her out, we tied one end of a rope to the baby's legs and the other to the bumper of our green pickup truck.

When it was all over, the mama cow ran off and never looked back. My mom and I wiped off the calf, then Mom gave me a piece of straw and showed me how to stick it in the calf's nose to make it sneeze and shake the mucus out.

In my mind I can see that calf, I can feel the rain, I can smell the wet mud. And for sure I can remember our shared feeling of having accomplished something powerful, and good. But for the life of me I cannot remember Mom's smile.

Farm kids are exposed to a lot growing up. We bottle-fed baby calves, we raised goats, sheep, pigs, chickens, ducks, turkeys—you name it, we had it. I witnessed the miracle of life many times, but I also witnessed the most awful of deaths—of animals, sure, but also of friends and neighbors, in car- and farm-related accidents. The two-lane road in front of our farm connected to a major highway through Kansas. There was no light at that intersection, and on too many nights, there were horrible car wrecks. We were nearly thirty miles from town, so every time we heard an accident, my family ran out and stayed with the injured people waiting for an ambulance. Back then, the ambulance was from the funeral home and had only one person in it, and that was the driver. You were pretty much shit out of luck once they loaded you in it.

Right across the main road was the school that served kindergarten to sixth grade. Before I was old enough to start, I would dig a hole under our yard fence and run across that dangerous highway so I could hang out with all the kids on the playground. The principal would always take me in his office and call Mom and say, "Joe is back at school today; would you like to come get him?"

Mom would come get me and take me home and pile bricks and dirt in the hole under the fence. I remember so badly wanting to go to school, and I remember everything about kindergarten, including the bright orange rug I took naps on. I especially remember standing in line waiting to pee. Some kids never made it to the bathroom.

We were surrounded by animals all the time, but a lot of farm kids are. The first dog I had was a toy Manchester named Frisky. Me and that dog was best friends. When I was in kindergarten, Dad got a Saint Bernard. I was in school when Dad went to the train to pick him up. We were having show-and-tell day, and Dad brought him in to surprise me. I can vividly see Dad walking down the sidewalk with that big white, brown, and black dog on a leash. I was so excited to meet that dog!

My true animal hobby began in earnest once I started grade school. Over summer break, I brought home the school's white mice and by summer's end, I ended up with hundreds of mice. After that, GW and I were in 4-H and FFA, and we spent our nights going around to different barns, catching pigeons and barn owls. At one point we had over five hundred pigeons. GW and I would show our pigeons, and take chickens and different animals to the local fair. You bet it was hard to raise something, show it, and know it might go to slaughter. Some people just bought them as pets to give the kids money for their projects.

The entire time I was growing up in Kansas until the age of thirteen, I used to bring home every stray dog there was. People from town made a habit of dumping off dogs at the farm, so I always had a steady stream of dogs to claim as mine. I guess they thought they'd be giving their dogs a better life, out on a farm. It never lasted long. Any adult dog I brought home, Dad would take it out and shoot it.

I told you my father was a mean man, and I meant it. It was devastating to me. If a litter of puppies was dropped off at the farm, which happened more than once, Dad would put them in a gunny sack and hold them underwater with a shovel until air bubbles quit coming up. He saw it as a practical matter; better they die now than slowly starve to death. Every time it happened, a part of my childhood was ripped from me.

When I was in sixth grade, Dad won some contest for selling corn, which came with a trip for two to Honolulu, Hawaii. There was no way he could take it because of work, but he let Mom go. GW and I both wanted to go real bad, because we wanted to see all the exotic jungle animals. In the end, GW got the plus-one. I understood; GW was the good kid. I was the one who accidentally burned down a field one time.

GW called when they got there and was all upset. "Honolulu

has no jungle," he said. "It's just a big, hot city." That was a real letdown to him and he'd spend the rest of his life talking about his wish to see the real jungles, with real animals, and the real indigenous people who lived among them.

While Mom and GW were gone, I fell on the sidewalk in front of the house and broke my arm. Dad didn't care; he made me go to school with a broken arm for three days before Mom came home and took me to the doctor. This was the first of many casts and injuries I would deal with in my life.

What I'm about to tell you I've never told anyone in my life, and I can only say it now because my dad is no longer here to deal with the shame and all his brothers and sisters are gone as well.

My father abused me, in every possible way a child can be abused. I remember sitting in his pickup truck out in the field, with no one around to help me, and he'd make me touch his penis. This happened many times. I'm sure you don't want to let your mind go there any more than I do. I felt completely helpless, nowhere to run and no one to help me.

I don't know if my siblings endured what I did. I don't know if Mom knew or not. However, soon after my dad started in on me, my brother Yarri began sexually abusing me as well. Yarri used to take me in the bathroom, pull a bottom drawer out to block the door, and make me have sex with him. Yarri kept on abusing me, for several years, until we left Kansas.

Since I have been imprisoned, a BBC documentarian named Louis Theroux sat down with my brother Yarri and asked him about whether he'd sexually abused me. Yarri denied it, but my memories are my memories. I have memories burned into my head that most people will never have to endure. For someone who's seen the things I've seen, having a photographic memory is less a blessing than a curse.

The sexual abuse Dad put me through ended around the time I was eight, but he continued to beat on me. Dad's rages always came with a high quantity of spit running out of his mouth and into your face. Him and Mom fought every day, and Yarri would often get into the mix, too. If Dad and Yarri were going at it, there was a good chance they'd start swinging at each other. GW was good at staying out of Dad's way, but I was always pissing Dad off.

One night, Dad was mad at me about something I'd done (I'm not blameless, I'm sure it was something stupid), and he held me down on the couch, choking me.

GW walked in right as Dad was wringing my neck. It was clear on his face that GW had had enough; he screamed as loud as he could for Dad to stop. "I swear I will never hit my kids—I'm going to break this abusive cycle!" he cried out.

Dad let me go and sulked his way outside, his pride hurt. GW had never stood up to him before. That was the last time Dad ever laid hands on me. GW was my hero.

# CHAPTER 2

**M**om and Dad bought Yarri a bright yellow Ford Mustang Mach 1 for his graduation. Tammy got a small orange car, and took off to live with her boyfriend. When it was GW's turn to get a vehicle, we drove out to Dodge City with Dad to pick it up. It was a brand-new white Chevy pickup with a camper shell. GW was happier than Christmas morning.

On the way out of town, GW and I were sitting at a red light in the new truck, the radio blasting some old country song. To our right was a cattle semitrailer. I remember thinking, *Wouldn't it be funny if one of those cows shit on our car?* Then it happened. *Splat.* A cow just shit green diarrhea from out the side of the semi, all across the hood of GW's brand-new white truck.

GW was a softhearted guy, and this was enough to make him cry. But he didn't scream or get overly upset.

"Doesn't that just make you nuts?" I said. "It's like God's out to get us!"

"God's not so petty," GW said. "No use being mad at life."

When we finally got to wash it off, the cow shit had left a per-manent green stain on the white paint. Surely it would have driven a lesser man absolutely apeshit.

GW could keep his cool, but working on the farm was hard on all of us. Then one year Dad went to a big horse sale in Den-ver, Colorado, and bought a stud named Market Price and hired a trainer.

In Market Price's first race, the odds were ninety-nine to one. I bought a three-dollar ticket for Market Price to come in third, and Dad bought a ten-dollar one for him to win. Market Price won his first race by almost two horse lengths; then he won nearly every race he ran in Denver and Ruidoso down in New Mexico.

Dad was hooked. With his newfound earnings, he bought a cattle ranch in the mountains of Centennial, Wyoming.

Wyoming gave me the best childhood memories. Our ranch lay at the foot of Centennial Ridge, and we had our own mountain, which we called Hogback Mountain, because of its shape. GW and myself spent nearly every waking hour on horseback, checking on cows and riding in the mountains. There were two horses: a big blue roan gelding named Smoky and a paint mare named Babe. Smoky I'd ride the most; Babe would lie down in the water every time we crossed a river.

One night right at dusk on the new property, GW let out a scream. I rushed outside and he ran up to me, saying, "I just saw Bigfoot, on the top of the hill, walking toward the mountain!"

GW never lied about anything, so if he said he saw something I never doubted him. From then on we kept one eye open at all times for Bigfoot. Some people might think that's crazy, but a few other townspeople said they saw Bigfoot the same night. It was a phenomenon people in that area claimed to see often.

You want to talk about the Wild West? At the age of thirteen I went on my first real cattle drive in Wyoming, driving two hundred cows around the mountains, from one ranch to another. It would take a couple days at a time. If it rained we'd have to plug holes in our tents with socks just to stay dry. Real Grizzly Adams kind of living. Life was good.

At our ranch, when calves were born, we'd have to work the herd so they could graze up the mountain on BLM land. That is Bureau of Land Management, not Black Lives Matter. BLM assigns you a certain amount of government land each year for your cattle to graze on. We would have to brand them so people knew they were our cattle, and we would cut the male calves to make them steers, so they didn't inbreed and would gain weight better. This was all done Old West style: the older guys would rope them on horseback and stretch them out. GW and I would castrate the bull calves and throw their testicles right on the open fire. Put a little salt on them and eat them right there. Mountain oysters, they're called. The texture could be like chicken or fish, depending on how well you cooked them. I couldn't eat them if they were mushy, so I always had to cook them well-done.

In the winter all the roads would close, so we had to ride a snowmobile to school. After classes, we'd go skiing at the resort just up the road. I did a lot of drinking back then. When you live in the mountains and the roads are closed with twenty-foot snowdrifts, all there is to do is play pool and drink. It can lead to trouble. I was an alcoholic when I was fourteen.

In the summer we'd ride horses or dirt bikes up on the mountain, on deer and elk trails under the aspen trees, across small creeks loaded with beaver dams. The best drinking water in the world was from a creek that came down the mountain—that taste you could never experience anywhere else. Sometimes me and GW would take the dams apart so the creeks would run better, and those damn beavers would work all night, chopping trees down and moving them into place. They'd have everything built and put back together the very next day.

Prairie dogs were everywhere too; they tore up the pasture and dug holes that cows and horses would trip in and break legs. Dad had Yarri shooting any prairie dog he saw, so me and GW came up with a plan to save them. There were three large trout lakes that flooded into each other and the middle one had an island in it. We made a raft just like on *Gilligan's Island* and set sail for "Prairie Dog Island," where we kept and fed all the ones we could catch. At one time we had over two hundred prairie dogs there.

I always loved animals, and continued bringing home every weird animal I could find. Caught my first porcupine, and a raccoon, which I bottle-raised and named Curiosity. Dad was deathly afraid of him and Curiosity knew it; he'd chase Dad all over the place. My little sister found an orphaned baby antelope, which I helped her raise. I also got a new dog, a mutt wirehair terrier named Onion. Onion's hair stood straight up like he'd stuck his tongue in a light socket. Man, he got run over so many times. A tough little dog. GW got a blue heeler named Misty, and she got caught in a coyote trap and lost one back leg. Poor thing, but she could still herd cattle that way. There's something real special about the bond between a boy and his dog.

Once I began junior high, people started picking on me for being different. By this time I hated school so bad. I never really had that many guy friends; hung out with girls most of the time. I knew something wasn't right because even then I had a crush on Rory, the boy from the ranch across the river. I did my best to have a girlfriend because that was the way it was supposed to be. I had a few girlfriends I hung out with. They knew I hated being who I was, even if they didn't know the reason.

I had some of the best friends in Wyoming, too. Jeff Peterson and his parents had a dude ranch down the road where people would vacation and go on horse trail rides. And I had a friend named Melinda Sharrard, the tomboy of Centennial, Wyoming, who lived in a trailer house there in town. She was a lot of fun; we were always in trouble and doing dangerous things. We both had motorcycles and went up the mountain for rides and raised hell. I think the worst we'd ever done was tent rolling, which is something of a sport in the mountains of Wyoming. Late at night we would go up to the campsites and get on each corner of a tent, pull up the stakes, and roll the tent so the poor saps inside would not be able to find the door. Then we'd stand in the bushes and watch them freak out.

There was an old, abandoned mine shaft we would spend a lot of time around. A tiny vein of gold went through the front of it: fool's gold. We never had the guts to go that far into the mine shaft. Bears were likely living inside, from what we could tell. I never saw a bear in the wild the whole time we lived up there, but they sure came down at night looking for food. One night I left the top of the barn door open and a bear got in and ate all my pet rabbits. You could follow its bloody tracks as it wandered around the yard, right next to the bedroom windows of the house.

Hunting in Wyoming is much different than how they hunt in Oklahoma and Texas. We'd spend days following tracks, learning about what we were hunting.

The first antelope I ever shot was a big buck, at the foot of Centennial Ridge. I shot it in the ass, of all places, which knocked it down, but I had to go get my dad to help me. I didn't know what else to do—hell, I was thirteen years old, and this antelope was down on its back going in circles with just its front legs.

Dad came up to the top of the pasture with me and shot it in its heart so it would die quickly. Then we packed it down to the shop, where we butchered it and put all the meat in the freezer. We sent the head to get mounted in Laramie, Wyoming. I found it too depressing to look at, but GW cherished it, and promised to always keep it with him.

That was a horrible experience. I started target practicing so it would never happen again.

When I shot my first elk I was with Yarri. I shot a young bull and it slid all the way down to a small creek that ran through the mountains, so we had to hike down to get it. Problem was, we got hopelessly lost on the way back. I thought we were dead for sure, eating snow to try to stay hydrated and then puking from eating too much snow. We finally found a cabin that was built just for people who'd gotten lost. It was stocked with cans of pork and beans and stuff, so we at least got to eat before starting back out from the bottom of the mountain. Two days later we finally got home with our freshly butchered elk, and that was my last trip hunting big game. From then on my mission was to find orphaned babies and raise them as pets until they decided to run off to return to the wild.

Never again did I return to hunting after I left Wyoming, but not because I don't believe in it—animals such as deer do have to be culled or they overpopulate and get diseases. It's just not my cup of tea after being able to connect and bond with animals like I do.

Growing up in the mountains like that is as close to living in the days of cowboys and Indians as it gets. You are never just a kid or a teenager; everyone treats you like an adult. I worked at the local restaurant, I herded cattle on cattle drives, and when I wanted to join the volunteer fire department, I did exactly that.

I got my emergency first aid license so I could work on the one ambulance we had in Centennial. My school bus driver was the fire chief, so he got me on the fire department and taught me so much about fires and how to drive the fire truck, even though our fire truck was an old army tanker with red lights that went about thirty miles an hour at full speed. The truck carried about five thousand gallons of water and had a lift pump on the back with a two-and-a-half-inch fire hose running off of it. The siren was controlled by a button on the floor you had to keep stepping on to make the sound go up and down.

I fought my first forest fire at fourteen years old. It was in Cheyenne, Wyoming—about 130 miles away. Our fire truck tanker was so old and slow it took two days to get there, but you bet your ass we made it and fought that fire, for nearly a week. Slept on the bare ground, using our helmets as pillows. The old firemen treated me no different than if I had been forty instead of fourteen. They contributed greatly to my understanding of how to treat others with respect.

# CHAPTER 3

Dad was getting into the racehorse business, full steam ahead. He bought a horse ranch in Texas, and moved us there. We drove down in a gooseneck horse trailer, packed full and strapped tight, just like *The Beverly Hillbillies*.

We landed in Pilot Point before our new house was ready to move into, so we all hunkered down in the equipment shop. Mom, Dad, and my baby sister, Pam, slept on a trampoline by the horse. Us three boys slept on mattresses on the floor. At night, we could feel armadillos digging in the ground under us. You know I just *had* to have one of those! I got my first parrot at that time, a blue-fronted Amazon named Taco. He got a bad cold and died.

Life is so crazy. We finally got to move into the new house—eight bedrooms, nine baths, just south of town with a horse ranch. Everyone in Pilot Point thought we were the new rich kids in town. Boy, was that a fucking mistake. Dad always had lots of land, big houses, and money to buy a new horse ranch and racehorses and shit, but we struggled and worked for what we had.

The jocks at school really fucked with me, calling me a fag and all that. Everything was all about football to them, and I was the new "rich" kid in town, hanging out with all the girls.

Though I didn't have the physical strength to be able to knock them down, I did get even with them in my own way. You know those roofing nails that are flat, with two prongs on one side? I took a whole case and lined the main drag of the school parking lot with them. Four hundred–plus flat tires and two cop cars later, they realized it was in their best interest to leave me alone.

Junior year of high school, I joined a band and met a girl named Jodi. I just knew Jodi was gonna save me from being gay. But in what was becoming a recurring theme, I was more attracted to her ex-boyfriend than I was to her. That relationship went to shit.

I met another girl named Lisa from a town close by. She was the only woman I ever had sex with, but I knew she'd be my last. Not because of anything wrong with her—I was the one who had the problem. I resented her for not being what I wanted her to be. We only had sex once. It just done nothing for me.

Somehow I made it to senior year of high school. I had too many credits but they wouldn't let me graduate early, so I took that year to attend community college and become an emergency medical technician (EMT). That's how at eighteen years old I had a job working on the Pilot Point ambulance. Within the next year, I was running my own ambulance business, servicing Sundial Manors Nursing Home. Mom was my business partner, as she would be for every business I've had since.

My sisters and Yarri stopped talking to me right about then. They thought I saw myself as some hotshot because I was making something of myself while it seemed to me they were content to be poor white trash all their lives. The only one doing anything with their life was GW. He'd met a girl named Lois soon after we moved to Texas. I remember the night he was going to propose to her, I sat with her and sang, "I know something you don't know."

I got so drunk and sick at their wedding. I was only seventeen and it was the last time I ever really drank liquor. GW and Lois moved a trailer in on my parents' ranch because he never wanted to leave Mom and Dad. He was dead set that they would never go to a nursing home, no matter what.

GW was living the married life, having kids and doing his own thing. I decided I needed to do my own thing, too, and get some distance between me and the family. I moved down to Eastvale, Texas, about fifty miles from my parents in Pilot Point.

Despite what my siblings thought, I was not leading a glamorous life. I will never forget a house fire I got called to in Little Elm, a town next to me. When I drove up, a fireman was chopping a hole in the side of a trailer house, and then pulled a man out. That man was burned over every part of his body, screaming for his children, even though his tongue was so burned it was swollen out of his mouth. After getting him to the hospital to fly to Dallas, we returned to the house just in time to see the coroner pour his two kids into a body bag. They'd been found in the kitchen sink, where they'd tried to put themselves out. A sight that haunts me to this day. People don't respect enough what first responders have to live with.

One of the guys I went to school with went on to be a cop, and he'd take me on rides sometimes. It was exciting; I felt like I could save the world as a cop. He was dating the daughter of the mayor of Eastvale, and it just so happened Eastvale was looking for a new cop. He told me if I liked riding with him so much, I should just get a badge and gun of my own.

Eastvale City Council wasn't having it. They said to me, "Joe, you look twelve. How can you handle yourself on the street?"

I offered them a deal: "Let me have the job, with no pay, for six months. If I prove myself, you guys hire me." Six months later, I graduated from the police academy as the youngest police chief ever in the history of the state of Texas. I wore a Smith & Wesson Model 66, .357 Magnum, a gun I would wear for the rest of my free life.

My time as a police officer gave me an inside look at just how corrupt our government can be. Here's an example of what I mean: One night I pulled over a man on suspicion of drunk driving. He wobbled his way through a field sobriety test, then refused a breath test. I arrested him for DUI.

This citizen, well within his rights, took his case to trial. The assistant district attorney called me into her office and went over what she was going to ask me when I testified. She said she would ask how visibly drunk the man was, and that I should respond by going on about how he was falling-down drunk, and that his driving was excessively erratic when I pulled him over.

Do you get what I'm saying to you? She wanted me to lie under oath and exaggerate his level of drunkenness to ensure a conviction. I refused to do that. This was a lawyer who worked for the county DA, not my city DA, and I was under no obligation to lie for her sake. I told the truth. The man got convicted anyway (he got probation) and I never again got called to testify for a case in Denton County.

The way I saw it, being a cop meant I was going to stand up for the helpless, and for the next few years, that's what I did. Protected the city as police chief and helped fight fires. I even got into a relationship with the fire chief's daughter, Kim Evens. It seemed like I had finally overcome all the inner turmoil I'd gone through.

Kim had two baby boys, neither with a father in the picture. Before we started dating I was already well aware I was gay, but I was fighting it down with all I had. And at first, it seemed like Kim was a woman who could make me straight. There was one problem: we'd never had sex, and I had no intention of consummating this relationship.

Eventually Kim figured out what was going on. But the crazy thing is, we got along so well that she didn't seem to mind. Kim was understanding of my predicament: I had to put on this front, being a police chief and all. Of course, she had her own predicament: trying to keep a stable home life for herself and her two kids. She was willing to play along with my make-believe life if I'd be willing to play my part in hers.

Kim and the boys moved into my trailer house with me up on the hill on the east side of Eastvale. Kim cooked, cleaned, and was my best friend. I took care of her boys as if they were my own, but even though I smiled my way through it, I was dying inside. I knew I was living a lie, and it wasn't fair to Kim and these kids to have to carry this lie for me. What would happen when they grew up and realized I was not their real dad and that I was gay on top of that?

Finally I'd had enough. I told Kim to take the kids and go get a life. I hated myself so much because it was entirely my fault. Kim did nothing wrong; she was more than great to me. I mean, hell, who would want to live with someone and never have sex?

You have to remember, this was the 1980s. In the gay district of Cedar Springs in Dallas, Texas, you didn't get caught walking the streets by yourself back then or you got beat up or killed. Rednecks would drive around town looking to gay bash for sport, literally hunting gays down on the streets. These homophobes hated us—*hated*—though often it was their own repressed homosexual desires they feared.

My brother Yarri knew I was gay, and he resented my trying to hide it with Kim. Yarri also couldn't stand that I was a police chief. And so I suppose it's for those reasons that when I left Kim, Yarri told my dad that it was because I was gay.

This did not go over well. Mom called me up and told me I needed to come by the house right away. I could tell in her voice that she knew I was gay, and that Dad knew, too, and that my entire world was about to fall apart.

I drove over to Mom and Dad's house in my police car, still in uniform. Dad came to his front door screaming, yelling, calling me a fag, spit flying from his mouth, same as it always did when he was mad. Mom was just standing behind him crying.

"You are a disgrace to the Schriebvogel name," Dad said. Then he grabbed my hand, shook it, and said, "Promise me, here in front of your mother, that you will not come to my funeral."

I got back in my car and drove off, crying the way you cry when your worst nightmare comes true. I had spent my life up to that point trying to avoid having that exact confrontation with my father. Why was I gay? What went wrong in my life that made me gay? Was it the abuse I suffered at the hands of my family? Did that mean I was going to be a helpless, broken man just like I'd been a helpless little boy?

The ride back to Eastvale was fifty miles of hard thinking.

What was the point of this struggle to live the life others wanted me to live, since I couldn't live the life I wanted? This was no life worth living. I made it back to the north side of the city limits, and then, in the blink of an eye, I drove my police car headfirst into a bridge wall.

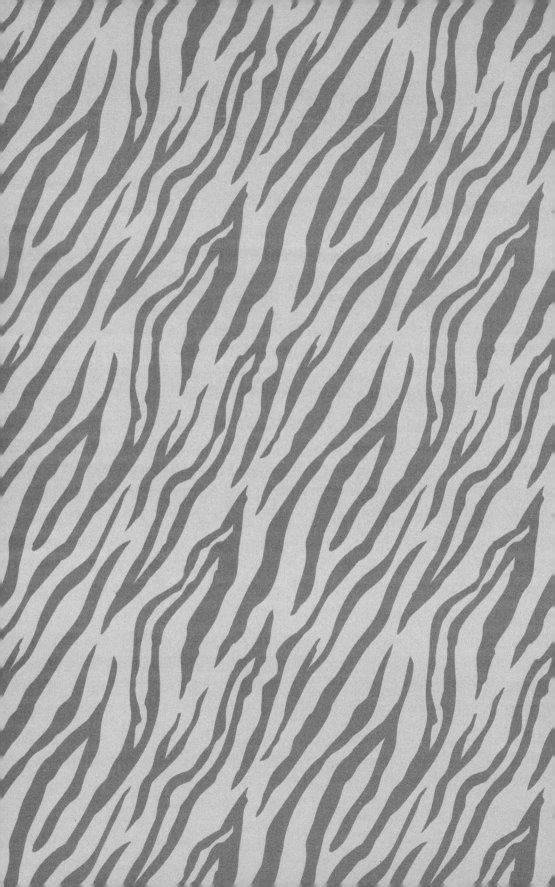

# CHAPTER 4

I remember being in excruciating pain. Some of the cops that worked for me were there at the scene of the crash, and so was Kim's dad, the fire chief. They picked me up in my own ambulance and took me to Medical City Dallas, where I spent nine days in a drug-induced coma. I'd broken my back and both my legs, on top of a concussion.

While I was in the coma, I could hear and see everything around me. A couple of guys I'd met at a bar came to see me, to support me. On the day I woke up, one of them, named Gregg Bass, was there. He brought me a steak and a baked potato and spent the night at the hospital with me.

For the next fifty-seven days I was in full-body traction. That meant I didn't get out of bed, for any reason, for two whole months. When I was finally able to get up, I moved in with Gregg in Dallas, until we decided to get the hell out of Texas, for a while at least, and relocated down to West Palm Beach, Florida, to continue my rehabilitation.

My life in West Palm Beach was nice; I did saltwater therapy for my broken back and legs and spent most every day on the beach. Gregg helped me, even when I was too proud to ask for it. It was the first time I had lived with a man, and while there were real problems in our relationship, I felt I could be myself around him, which was nice. We had a neighbor in West Palm Beach who managed a store, Pet Circus, and I'd go diving daily to catch saltwater fish for them to sell. It was a way to make some extra cash, and eventually I got a job working in the store.

So much in my life had gone wrong to lead me to that car accident. But God most definitely works in mysterious ways because it was in Florida that I found my true calling. One of the employees at Pet Circus also worked at Lion Country Safari, and he'd bring home baby lions and monkeys every night that needed to be bottle-fed.

There's a lot of controversy out there about whether it's inhumane to take a baby away from its mother and bottle-feed it, but what I learned at this time was that it is just about the only way to ensure these big cats are able to live peacefully among human beings. Big cats are some of the most dangerous animals in the world, but when you learn how to communicate with them and they register your scent at an early enough age, they'll imprint on you and you end up with much tamer animals in captivity. Big cats don't have the freedom and luxury to walk around the earth unencumbered, so the only options are living a tame life or going extinct, or worse yet, living a life in a cage with no interaction whatsoever.

I got the most amazing sense of affection from those babies; they'd eat, then curl up in my lap and fall asleep. I was hooked on exotic animals from that moment on. But I was also learning how to make money in the animal world. I started managing Pet Circus, and next thing I knew I had about forty-five parrots living in my garage, and I was selling them on the side.

After a year in Florida, Mom wanted me to come back home. I missed her and GW real bad, but I was conflicted. Going to Florida wasn't just about mending my body; I'd needed to mend my broken mind, which was filled with so much self-hatred.

Even though my relationship with Gregg wasn't working out, being with him had taught me so much about myself. I'd learned to live with my depression, a struggle I still fight with to this day. I had a new lust for life, and I didn't want to waste any more of my time on this earth being miserable in the closet.

There was part of me that felt the need to prove the world wrong about being gay. I wanted to be the biggest and the best at everything and anything I did so I could show the world that a gay man can outdo any straight person out there. And if anyone had a problem with that, it was their problem, not mine.

I asked Mom if she still wanted me back even if I was going to live my life openly as a gay man. Mom told me she loved me and that she'd accept me no matter what I did in life. Then she got GW on the phone, and he told me he loved me, too. That made me cry. We'd never really discussed my sexuality before, and even though I knew my brother loved me and in my heart I knew he'd accept me, part of me always worried that he'd treat me differently when he found out I was gay. To my immense relief, he surely didn't.

I can't say the same for all my family. My sisters and Yarri wanted nothing to do with me, and Dad wouldn't talk to me, either. Mom did get him to buy me a mobile home, and I agreed to accept that charity, with one condition: I wanted to pick where it'd go. That's how I ended up in Arlington, Texas, about twenty miles outside Dallas and a good two-hour ride from my parents, who now lived in Springer, Oklahoma. Close enough to see each other, but far enough away that I could establish my own life. That was the only way I could ever be happy.

GW and Mom came down to help me and my forty-five parrots and get us all situated. The first thing I did when I got to Arlington was find myself a job, doing security at a bar in Dallas: the Round-Up Saloon. The Round-Up is a country-and-western gay bar with a large dance floor and a bar on each side, separated with glass windows so you can sit and watch people dance. It also has a large outdoor patio where you can go smoke.

My main job as security was working the door and checking IDs. And that's right where I was one night when I first met the man I'd be married to for the next sixteen years: Brian Rhyne.

Brian was all country and western, and wore the look well. A good-looking guy and very bright, I could tell from the moment I met him. I said hello and I'm sure I seemed foolish, but he smiled and we connected.

I saw him a few more times at work, and then I came in on a night off and there he was. I asked him if he wanted to dance with me and he said yes. Turned out Brian was going to school during the day to learn to cut hair. I asked him if he'd cut mine and he laughed and said he gladly would because my hair was a mess.

We met up a few more times after that night, and he did indeed cut my hair, giving me my signature mullet, which was the envy of all who saw it. Then one night I went to his place just off Interstate 75 in Dallas, and we slept together. This was the first time I'd ever truly loved someone like this and it was the greatest feeling in the world. Within two weeks of meeting, Brian moved into my trailer with me. Two months later, we got married on the patio at the Round-Up.

This wasn't a legal wedding or anything, but it wasn't about legality—it was about committing to this bond in a formal way. The owner of the bar decorated the place and built an arch for us to get married under. My parents weren't there, but Brian had three friends stand on his side and I had three on mine. It was more than I ever could have hoped for, but all that really mattered was I finally had the love I wanted so badly.

Brian cleaned, cooked, and took care of me. I never wanted for anything. He loved his family; we'd go out to his mom's in Oklahoma every few weeks. She lived right on a beautiful creek and we'd have cookouts, with Brian out there on the grill, making sure everyone was happy and full. It was all about the simple life with Brian. His people were all so peaceful, unlike anything I'd ever experienced in my own family.

I got promoted to bartender at the Round-Up, and Brian got a job cutting hair in the Winn-Dixie shopping center in Arlington. It just so happened there was a big old pet store in there called Pet Safari, owned by a sweet old couple named Sandy and Stanton Kizer. They ran a nice little business there but were looking to retire. I saw this as a fantastic opportunity to really make my mark in the world.

I went to Mom and told her I wanted to buy the store. Mom said she thought it was a good idea but gave me one condition: she wanted my brother GW to co-own the business with me, and come down and help me run it.

This was just about the best news I could hope for. Me and GW happily became business partners.

With Brian working a few doors down from me, we worked and lived every breath together. GW drove down almost every day and would stay at our house a couple times a week. We opened the store at 7 a.m. and closed at nine every night, so there was not much time to do fun things, but the three of us got along great.

Our business was a huge success. GW built all the cat furniture, dog houses, and reptile cages we sold, and then he started selling that stuff to almost every pet store in the Dallas–Fort Worth area. Things were going so well that we took over an old nursery store in the shopping center and expanded from 1,400 square feet to 40,000. We changed the store's name to Super Pets and got a new logo flag out near our street sign, with a dog wearing a cape. At our busiest, we employed thirteen full-time groomers, and groomed about 110 dogs a day. We took our luck and passed it on by helping people. One-dollar dog baths to raise money for charity was the main way we gave back.

For the most part, the people in Arlington were awesome. Kerry Von Erich, a.k.a. The Texas Tornado, of professional wrestling fame, hung out at the pet store a lot because he was friends with one of the groomers. Terry Dorsey, the morning radio show guy, was a real good customer and friend. Bobby Valentine from the Texas Rangers was also a good customer, as was his wife. They had four huge collies that they brought in all the time to have groomed.

One of the most fun things we did at the store was wildlife rescues and removals. We lent out live traps to catch skunks and raccoons in town, and GW and I would take them out in the country, away from car traffic, and release them.

When a customer called us to pick up a trap with a skunk in it, we'd take big sheets of plastic and hold them out in front of us as we approached the trap. The skunk would try to spray us as we got close, leaving yellow stains on the plastic. We'd keep on approaching and eventually wrap the skunk up in the plastic like a stinky Christmas present. Then we'd strap it to the roof of our truck and put on our rotating yellow hazard lights.

The smell was something fierce. As we drove skunks out of town, people would give us their worst "go to hell" looks. But when they'd look to see who was driving, they'd find GW and me, smiling and singing along to the radio, blaring "Purple Rain" by Prince, "Karma Chameleon" by Boy George, or anything by Selena, who was my idol. Pissed-off people usually started laughing once they saw us. These wildlife rescues brought in so much business because people respected us for what we did for the animals.

I felt like I was finally living the life I was meant to live. That doesn't mean everything was perfect—far from it. As much as I loved Brian, we had some major issues—issues that were affecting a lot of gay men our age.

Gays had come so far, but many of us still hold on to self-hatred. This makes the gay community especially vulnerable to drug abuse, specifically to the drug crystal meth.

If you've ever done meth, you will relate to this, but for those who don't know, let me tell you just how this shit can ruin lives and fuck your head up. Meth has the power to destroy any relationship. Meth makes people do stupid things, and they generally have no idea how stupid they're acting because they're too high to maintain any level of self-awareness.

In the early nineties I experimented with meth with Brian. He liked it a lot more than I did. It's an especially addictive substance, and I hated feeling like that—I didn't even like the way drinking made me feel—but Brian's addiction was stronger, too strong for him to control. Once we tried it, every weekend became party time for Brian with crystal meth. He'd go to the park or the lake or one of the bathhouses in Dallas and pick up tricks.

Brian was a much more sexual person than I was. Who was I to stop him from doing what made him happy? I remember thinking, *We are gay men; we don't need to be confined by straight people's standards of what a relationship is.* But truthfully, I didn't believe my own bullshit, and I knew it was my own poor self-esteem that allowed Brian to keep on doing the things he did. I don't want to be judgmental, but I'm not some slut. That's just me.

It got to a point where me and Brian were no longer having sex. It was always Brian with someone else while I watched. Even though I didn't like watching, I wouldn't allow Brian to do it unless I was there. People get sloppy when they're on meth, so I always wanted to make sure they stayed safe and wore protection. I felt like I had to.

In 1994 we found out that Brian was HIV-positive. His viral load was so high they said he must have been positive since before we even met.

For gay men, this diagnosis was as bad as it gets. HIV was a death sentence. I was only thirty and Brian was about the same age, but we had already watched seven of our friends waste away and die from AIDS.

I was tested time and time again and never came up positive. Our doctor in Fort Worth struggled to come up with a reason for this, considering I'd been with Brian for so long. She eventually proposed two possible explanations: either I'd had so many rabies shots from getting pre-exposure vaccines that it could have somehow prevented my blood cells from being mimicked by HIV, or I was born into the 1 percent of the world population that has imperfect cells that can't mimic HIV. Some of my know-nothing relatives claim that I'm HIV-positive, but they're wrong, as are my relatives who think I have a child out there somewhere. I have nothing in my life to hide.

There was not much I could do to help Brian except support him and continue the commitment I'd made to him the day we'd married: to be with him "till death do us part." He started treatment, and honestly the medicine seemed to make him sicker than the HIV did, the same way chemo kills some cancer patients. But we stayed together, side by side every day, and though we didn't tell anyone Brian was sick, we began to do more dog-dip events at the store, to fundraise for AIDS charities. There wasn't much else we could do.

If you have a family member that comes out as gay, do yourself and them a huge favor: just accept them the way they are and move on in life. Don't make the same mistake my family did. People are who they are. No one ever sat on their deathbed thinking, *I shouldn't have accepted my son for being a queer*. Love and acceptance will see you through.

# CHAPTER 5

Despite the fact that the whole DFW area had a bad problem with gay bashings, I had a rainbow gift shop in the pet store, and it always did well. A couple times we had guys come in and have a problem with it, but usually it wasn't that big a deal. One day a guy yelled out about how we were a fag store, and even though it didn't bother me, it got GW real mad.

To make sure no one would again be confused about what our store stood for, my brother went out and painted our street sign with rainbow colors and took down our Super Dog flag and replaced it with a rainbow flag.

"Fuck 'em," GW said. "You're my brother and if they don't like it they can deal with me."

The city wrote us a warning letter, saying that we didn't have a flag permit for the rainbow flag and didn't have approval to be painting our own sign. I was not about to start putting up with this shit any more than GW was, so we went to the local news and told them we were being discriminated against. In March

1997, the *Dallas Morning News* ran a story about our store and the homophobia we were facing. Within three days we received a waiver to have the street sign and flag pole displaying whatever we wanted. I'll say it again, my brother was my hero.

My older sister, Tammy, wanted to move from up in Oklahoma down to Florida. Dad talked GW into driving her and moving her stuff. He stayed the night at my house, and the next morning in my front yard, GW shook my hand and said to me, "If anything ever happens to me, I have enough in CDs to keep Lois and the kids going for a while."

This wasn't something GW normally said. It was like he knew something was going to happen. About 6 p.m. that night the phone rang; it was Mom. She told me that GW and Tammy were in a bad wreck; they'd been hit by a drunk driver. Mom and Dad were on the way to pick me up.

"Is he going to be okay?" I asked.

"They don't think he's going to make it," she said.

It was the call you never want to get. We arrived at the hospital in Corsicana, Texas, to find GW just out of surgery from having his spleen removed. Both legs, his back, and neck were broken, and his head injury was so bad his eyes bulged out of their sockets. He was awake but on a ventilator and scared as hell. My brother knew he was going to die.

The doctors put GW in a drug-induced coma, and the waiting room is where we called home for the next seven days. They kept telling us he was brain-dead but I just couldn't accept that. I tried to set up a transfer to another hospital, but every time I got one set up, GW's doctor would tell them he was dead. No hospital would accept a dead body, so I made a deal with the devil. I told Baylor, a much nicer hospital, that I would donate GW's organs if they would take him and prove to me his brain was not working. They agreed.

All this was going on while Tammy was in another room dealing with over twenty-one fractures of her own. My oldest brother, Yarri, didn't skip a beat—I thought he was trying to get in all the nurses' pants while our brother and sister lay there. The rest of our family was devastated, just shaken to our core. Dad was at GW's hospital bed every day crying, not for GW—he was crying for himself because he had been such an asshole, and now his son was brain-dead and would never hear any apologies.

The time had come for GW's transfer. Dad was sitting on the grass outside the hospital, unable to cope. I sat down with him and told him the details about the transfer I'd set up. I told him that GW might still technically be alive but he wasn't there anymore. His urine was black from his kidneys shutting down. The sparkle in his eyes was dull. When you talked to him or touched him, his heart rate never changed; that meant he was truly gone.

The hurt and guilt were all over Dad's face. "I never got to tell him I loved him," Dad said. It was true: Dad had never said those words to any of us. His whole life he'd worried about nothing other than putting money in the bank for retirement and a rainy day, and GW never got to enjoy a dime of the money he'd saved. It just tore Dad up to think about, to the point he didn't want to be in this world anymore. He blamed himself for GW dying because it was Dad who had talked him into driving Tammy down to Florida, instead of just hiring someone to do it.

Dad wanted to kill himself. He told me he'd just drive into an oncoming semi, or go into a bar and piss someone off so maybe they'd shoot him. He raised us to believe that committing suicide would stop you from going to Heaven, but he thought if he got someone else to do it for him, God wouldn't judge him. I told Dad he was wrong, and if he did that, he would never get to see GW again. Dad would just have to live with his guilt the rest of his life.

Seeing my dad like that, just completely broken, I forgave him in my heart for all the wrong he'd done to me, to all of us. I forgave my dad not because he deserved forgiveness; I forgave him because my soul couldn't hold on to the pain anymore. I had to follow GW's example and be there for my father even though he'd never been there for me. I was going to have to step up and be the bigger man.

The helicopter arrived to move GW to Dallas and get him out of this hellhole they called a hospital, where, it seemed to me, people were dying from knee surgery. When the flight paramedics rolled GW out into the parking lot, the strangest thing happened: huge globs of spiderwebs fell from the sky, all over the helicopter. I don't know where they came from; I swear it was the silk curtains of Heaven as he passed through them.

When that happened, I knew GW's time on Earth was done, and that he'd made it up to Heaven. They took him to Baylor and proved there was no blood flow to his brain. On October 7, 1997, I said goodbye to my brother Garold Wayne Schreibvogel. He was thirty-two years old. The last thing I said to my brother were those three simple words: "I love you." It's doubtful he was able to hear me. But I told myself then that I would never leave someone without saying "I love you" to their face, no matter how mad I was or what was going on.

The funeral was a nightmare; it was held at a Catholic church and the priest couldn't pronounce GW's name correctly, which disgusted me. Even worse than that was having to keep Dad from finding out that we had donated GW's organs. I'd bribed someone in the coroner's office to put "visual autopsy" on the death certificate so Dad wouldn't know. Only myself, Mom, Yarri, and Lois knew the truth. It was a closed casket, and Dad kept throwing himself over it, and insisting they open it up. I got the funeral director to agree to say it couldn't be opened; I didn't want Dad to go through all this pain over and over again.

Yarri came up to me and Mom at the funeral, and told us he didn't think it was right we'd lied to Dad about the organ donation. He said he'd keep his mouth shut, for a price, and walked away. Mom and I just looked at each other and both started crying. How did I get one brother sent from Heaven and another sent from Hell? And why did God have to take the wrong one?

I called Yarri later on, when I had a moment of privacy. I let him know in no uncertain terms that the way he was with me when I was a kid was not simply lost in the past. Just because I'd kept it to myself all these years didn't mean I would continue to do so.

I think that scared him. From the day GW went into the ground I have not spoken to Yarri again. Only the unbearable loss of watching GW die could give me the strength to call Yarri out like that.

I found it very difficult to believe in anyone other than my brother Garold Wayne Schreibvogel. And as far as I know, he was a great dad who broke the cycle of abuse we'd suffered. There is so much one must endure to make it through life, and that is *if* you make it through life. GW was real—he did everything for everyone. I miss him so much and I know if he were still alive and we had the opportunity to build a zoo together, he would have helped build the best zoo there ever was. He would have been all-in on that.

I've since gone on to experience many more losses. What I've learned is, there are small signs all around us that the people who care about us the most are still there watching out for us. These signs can carry us through the toughest times there are. All you have to do is look out for them.

# INTERLUDE

Unbeknownst to me, on August 18, 1997, two months before GW died, another man died a tragic death. His name was Don Lewis and, according to his then-wife, Carole, he got up early for work that day and she never saw him again. The official report is that he went missing. But I believe Don Lewis was never really missing.

Me and my family were afforded at least one luxury in GW's death, and that is there's no denying what happened to him. As terrible as it was, there was no mystery to my brother's death, except the one great mystery of why God lets terrible things happen to good people.

Don Lewis's family is still waiting for that one luxury; they don't know what happened to their daddy. But they have a pretty good idea.

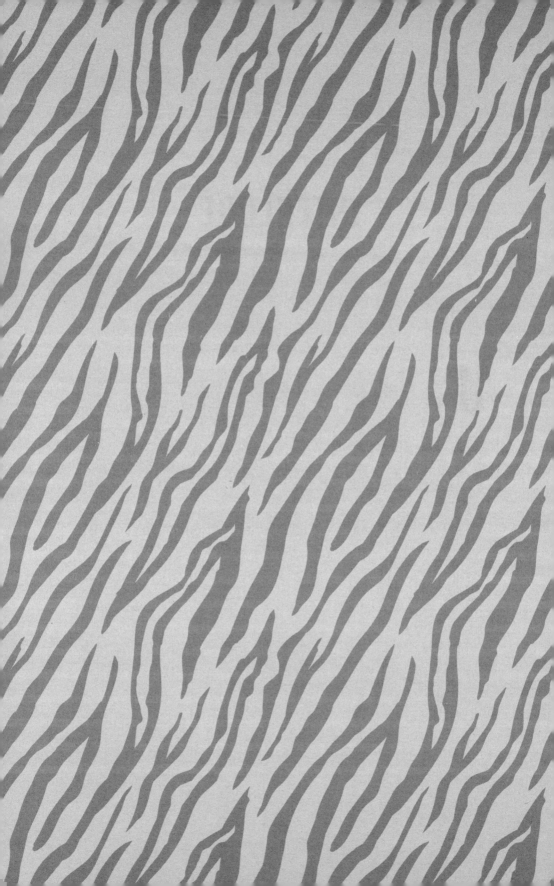

# CHAPTER 6

A lot of things changed after GW was gone.

I sold the pet store. It just wasn't the same anymore.

Dad suddenly became my biggest fan. He was calling me every day now. Never formally apologized for anything he'd done, but he showed it through support, and acceptance of Brian as my husband. Dad and Mom asked Brian and me to move back up to Oklahoma, closer to them. We both agreed. We were eager to get out of the Dallas–Fort Worth area.

GW had always stayed near my parents to help take care of them, and now I took on the responsibility. Dad had given up working with his horses after GW died and the ranch had gone to hell. I got out there and mowed and took care of things.

Things with Brian had changed a lot, too. He was starting to get sicker and quite often had a full-time PICC line in his arm for IV medications. He couldn't work anymore, but he also couldn't keep doing crystal meth, which was a small blessing. People are a lot easier to be around when they're not tweaking out on meth.

We'd made a commitment to each other, for better or worse, "till death do us part." It helped that I loved him. He was there for me, and sober, when GW died and I needed him most. Both of us were committed to seeing this thing through.

Mom and Dad got about $140,000 from the insurance for GW's death. It caused a lot of issues within our family. Both my sisters wanted a piece of that money. They felt entitled to it. Dad called it "blood money" and was adamant that no one would profit from GW's death. He wanted to donate it all to charity, which I was skeptical of, because I'd seen from my time in the pet stores that a lot of charities are really just big scams.

This is what gave me the idea. Mom told me she was having trouble taking care of the animals GW had left on their ranch. He'd had a pet red deer named Jingles and a big old buffalo. I thought, *What if we built a park, where we could take care of GW's pets, and rescue the animals GW had dreamed of seeing in the wild?* It could be a memorial to GW, but we could also allow other people to join in and memorialize their loved ones, too.

The more I thought about it, the more I loved it and was set on convincing my parents a memorial park was the thing to do. GW loved the jungle; he had been so upset when he'd gotten to Hawaii and there was no jungle. Now we could build him a jungle!

To get us started, we combined the insurance money with the money I'd made selling the store. Dad knew of a property for sale in Wynnewood, next to I-35, which had belonged to an old racehorse buddy of his. It was sixteen acres of open grassland, with a house on it, and a rodeo arena. Dad bought the land, and Brian and I moved into the house.

From then on, both my sisters disowned me and referred to my mother only by her first name, which made me see red. My sisters thought we were getting rich from the zoo, when in fact Mom and Dad and I put every dime we ever saved into it just to keep the doors open. If they only knew how hard we worked to build that place and what we gave up. We had to haul scrap iron just to pay the bills.

What my sisters did not realize is that Mom, Dad, and myself needed something, anything, to focus our heartbreak on. It's my true belief that the zoo is the only thing that kept the three of us from succumbing to our pain.

Building the first row of cages, which later became known as Tiger Alley, kicked our ass. There were days we just cried while putting it up because it was so hard. But no matter how hard it was, we never gave up. GW's red deer and his buffalo were our first inhabitants. The buffalo was addicted to peppermints and would follow you anywhere for one.

We had no large equipment to do anything, so it was all done by Mom, Dad, and me, with ladders and by hand. Brian was too sick by then to help outside. Dad would pick up nine tons of gravel at a time, and he and Mom would shovel it into wheelbarrows, which I'd push one at a time into the cages so the animals would be high off the ground when it rained. Then as we grew and more things got built, Dad brought up his small tractor and dug all the ponds on the zoo grounds for the rain to drain and the animals to have water to play in.

Word spread quickly that we were taking in animals that had nowhere else to live. Before we even got the first row of cages done, I got a call from someone who needed help. He said he had a mountain lion as a pet, but could no longer afford to take care of it and didn't know what to do.

I felt bad for the guy. There's a big difference between an animal that's been mistreated and needs to be rescued, and a situation like this where a guy got in over his head but was trying to do right by his animal. And of course, I was excited by the prospect of getting a mountain lion for the zoo. I told him I'd come down and check it out.

The cat's name was Sheba; she was seven years old, and beautiful, with a touch of gray all through her coat. Sheba had spent her life to that point living in an old grain silo. There was a cage within it that wasn't all that big, but she was in good shape and they fed and cared for her well. Her owner cried his eyes out as he helped me get her into the back of my pickup truck to haul her back to the zoo.

Now, keep in mind I was a complete stranger to this cat and had just hauled her two hundred miles away from her home. But for some reason, me and Sheba really just hit it off. She adored me; there was no attempt at aggression from her at all, which seemed odd to me. Aren't big cats supposed to be vicious man-killers? I had no idea. This is the crazy part: no one trained me to do any of this. I literally had no idea what I was doing.

Had I known anything about working with big cats, I surely would have been too scared to get in a cage with one that didn't know me. They say God protects babies and fools, and I guess GW had God looking out for me, because I was comfortable enough with Sheba to get in her cage to clean and feed her.

Sheba was a great cat. I got her to walk on a leash, and she'd drive in the passenger seat of my truck with me. Our relationship was like a man with his dog except it was a man with his mountain lion. It stayed that way until she died nine years later, at the age of sixteen.

Soon after we got Sheba, I was contacted by a man just a couple miles up the road who had a black bear that he wanted to place at the zoo. The bear's name was Boo. This man had gotten Boo when he was a cub, but now he was four years old and the situation was no longer sustainable.

When I went to see him, Boo was living in a cage, and there were four white kittens, maybe about three months old, that had been living in the cage with him. I loaded Boo up and brought him to the zoo. For nearly two weeks he wouldn't eat; he lay in his house and wouldn't come out. I tried everything I could to get that bear to get up and eat, but it got to the point where I thought he was going to die. I thought maybe he was missing his owner, so I called the guy and he came down and got Boo to come out and get on top of his house and perk up a bit. But as soon as he left, Boo went back into his seclusion.

Something wasn't right here. I tried to figure it out, and it was a long shot, but I thought: *What if that bear is missing those kittens?*

What made me think a bear could miss kittens, I do not know. The owner said it was worth a try, and brought the kittens down— and within one day, Boo was out eating and lying on top of his house with those little guys. They stayed with him until they grew up and crawled out of the cage. When they left, he did not go back into mourning for them; it was like he knew they needed to go and be cats at some point.

From then on, I became more Boo's friend than he did mine.

Anytime I brought a load of gravel into his cage to keep it dry, Boo the Bear would sit in the wheelbarrow and make me stop working so I would feed him marshmallows and rub the top of his head. He was too big to push around, but after he'd had enough of a sugar fix he would get out so I could go back to work.

It wasn't long after that I got a call from the Oklahoma game warden that someone had moved out of a subdivision south of Ardmore and left a pair of tigers, a mountain lion, and a black leopard. We hooked up the horse trailer and called a local vet, Dr. Green, to meet us there.

At the house, we found these animals had been left behind, and they had been there alone so long they were skin and bones and eating what garden hose they could pull through the cage. It was a sad sight indeed. Dr. Green sedated them and we loaded them in the horse trailer. We were in a rush to get to the zoo before the animals woke up because they were so bad off we couldn't give them more drugs to keep them asleep. Their bodies were too weak to handle it. The sheriff escorted us to the interstate with their red lights and siren on, and the highway patrol met us on I-35 and cleared the way for us back to the zoo.

The tigers were named Ramsey and Isis, and they were our first two tigers. We got them all unloaded and treated without incident, and soon enough we got them fattened up and looking great.

Because I had been able to interact so closely with Sheba, it made me feel like I could be friends with any animal. You know I should have been killed one thousand times, because when I cleaned their cages I'd lock myself in with them. I had to; there was no one else out there with me but Mom and Dad, and if something happened I couldn't risk the animals' getting loose. But they never hurt me, which was puzzling, but it also made me start to realize the connection I have with animals was maybe not normal. Like a superpower.

Ramsey and Isis had their first babies born at the zoo. Six in the litter, which is the largest litter possible for a tiger. Considering where they'd come from, I knew I was doing something right. I bred tiger cubs from then on.

Before the park was anywhere near open, we were already packing in all kinds of cool animals. But nothing could have prepared me for what would become known as The Great American Emu Rescue.

I'd gotten a call from the Red Oak Police Department in Texas. They had a man in custody for animal cruelty; he'd been starving his emus. The police had heard about me and what I was all about, and they wanted to know if I'd come down and help them deal with their emu problem.

I had never seen an emu in real life before, but how hard could it be to catch a big bird and put it in a trailer? I got some horse trailers and some guys to help out, and we went down to Red Oak.

For a while back there in the nineties, people thought they were going to get rich with emu meat and oil. Some of those birds were bringing in up to $20,000 each. Then the market fell out. People were turning them loose or just starving them because they didn't want to pay the money to feed them.

Let me tell you something about emus: these things are stupider than half the staff who ever worked at my zoo. We pulled up to this property and there were sixty-nine emus in this huge fenced-in area, running around in every direction with their necks bouncing back and forth. Trying to get to them was dangerous all on its own—they have three talons on each foot and those things are razor sharp.

We backed the trailers up to the gate in the fence and thought we were about to start catching these things. First we tried ropes and I roped one, which wasn't too hard to do, until he jumped ten feet up in the air. That's how we found out emus can kick, really hard. One of the volunteers got his leg sliced wide open. There were about six police cars there, so they called an ambulance and a fire rescue squad.

We switched tactics, and used some portable panels to push the emus toward the trailer on their own. That worked for about ten or fifteen emus, and then these dumb birds started jumping and walking across the top of each other, cutting open the backs of other emus. I couldn't believe what I had gotten myself into, but we were already there and we couldn't stop.

The fire rescue truck was staying busy just treating the growing number of injured volunteers, so the police brought the emus' owner out from jail in handcuffs to tell us how to catch these things.

"You have to ride their backs and steer them with their wings," he said.

Yeah, right, okay, so guess who was the first to try that? You got it: me. I caught this emu, got on its back, and grabbed these tiny little wings—and this thing ran me right into a tree, dislocated my right knee, and kicked me on the way down. Splayed my leg wide open.

The ambulance hauled me to the hospital, I got my knee put back in, forty-seven stitches in my leg, and a brace, and I got right back out there an hour later like the fool I am because it's never enough to just say *I quit*.

We finally were down to the last nine emus and these ones are all troublemakers, jumping the fence, getting on the interstate. The police chief was worried they were going to cause a wreck and kill someone. He said they needed to be put down.

I hadn't brought any guns—this was an animal rescue—so we got the town vet down there and she said, "Well, if you could catch them, we could euthanize them."

"If we could catch them to do that, we would just put them in the trailers!" I said.

The police chief said, "What if we shot them? Where would we need to aim to put them down fast and painless?"

She replied, "The biggest mass of the body."

A police officer opened the trunk of his car and handed me and another volunteer sawed-off shotguns, showed us how to use them, and said, "Here ya go, put them down."

I'd never had a cop hand me a gun before. Never did again, either. I shot the first emu, and have you ever heard the expression "Running around like a chicken with its head cut off"? Imagine what a prehistoric chicken looks like, flopping around on the ground gushing blood for ten minutes before it dies.

I was in shock as I put down each one of these things. All the while all this was going on, some people associated with the ASPCA out of Dallas, the actual animal people, were on hand, sitting in their van the whole day, doing nothing to help.

A couple days later I heard on the news that the ASPCA pressed charges on me for putting the nine emus down. I had to go face the grand jury in Red Oak, and thank God they were a bunch of little old men in overalls. I sat in there and cried in front of them and told them we came to a rescue with ropes and horse trailers, and that the cops gave us the guns and told us to put them down. They were like, "They did *what*?" The police officer who gave us the guns even stood up for us, so the grand jury "no billed" us, which means no charges were filed.

This was my first encounter with any animal rights groups and all I learned is the people who bitch about animal cruelty and raise money are often the same ones that never lift a finger to help rescue something.

A few months down the road I finally learned by accident how you get an emu to be calm. You squirt it with a garden hose and the dumbass birds just lie down in the water to let you spray them. Now you know.

# CHAPTER 7

On October 14, 1999, the second anniversary of GW's funeral, we officially opened the Garold Wayne Exotic Animal Memorial Park. When we opened I had four mountain lions, five tigers, a black leopard, a black bear, some ducks, chickens, one deer, sixty emus, GW's red deer and buffalo, and that was about it.

Mom and Dad were so proud of the zoo. They spent every day telling their story to people who had also lost a child or loved one. It helped everyone. That's what my brother stood for. People all over the world pitched in and sponsored memorials for their lost loved ones. We ended up with 152 memorials. My brother was famous around the world. I worked the next eighteen years for GW.

Boo the Bear and I got to know each other to the point that he and I would do this thing for customers, where he would walk down the steps of his house to the front of the cage and stand up on his hind legs. Then together we would walk back to his house and he'd get on top. All this for marshmallows! People loved watching me interact with him and the other animals.

Stuff like this is what made my zoo so much more special than any other place. We charged an entrance fee, but didn't do any shows or anything; I just spent all day long inside the cages, cleaning them and talking to the customers as they'd walk by. The public got to see the love and connection I had with my animals. They weren't being exploited for money—they were my kids, my family. I raised them that way. God knows just as many were in the house as in the zoo. Every baby born at the zoo lived in the house. Some grew up and never left the house. I didn't have to worry about someone breaking in at night because my children were my protectors as I was for them.

I never made a single one of my cats do a trick. For most big-cat owners it was or is about showing off. For me, it was about love, not a show, and they respected me as a family member. When I'd walk in a cage with fourteen cats at one time, I became a cat myself. The cats that wanted to be loved on came to me, and the ones that wanted to be left alone, I'd leave alone. Cats are just like us: they're just trying to survive, same as we are.

One of the only animals that really ever hurt me bad was the black leopard, named Bagheera. He was one of the cats I rescued with Ramsey and Isis out of Ardmore, Oklahoma. I was feeding him through the cage one day and he went to grab chicken and got my hand instead.

I knew it was bad. When I finally got my hand back, I put a tourniquet around my wrist and drove myself to the emergency room. They pulled my glove off, and my right thumb and index finger came nearly completely off with it. Thank God they were able to sew me back together and I went right back to building the zoo. We were building something almost every day.

As hard as it all was, building the zoo is what kept Mom and Dad not only alive but together. Angels were everywhere. It was amazing how people responded and joined in on the cause. Mom and Dad greeted guests, and got to spend time talking about GW, and meeting people who went through similarly traumatic losses.

The park kept expanding, as people just kept bringing animals one after another, calling me to come get tigers, until I had about the first twenty-five tigers I ever had. Just Mom and Dad and I did this, while Brian got sicker in the house.

Brian never got in with any of the animals other than the first baby camel we had gotten, whose name was Humphrey. One time Brian drove to Corpus Christi, Texas, and got a load of tigers and a bear from a place called Wayne's World, and one of the tigers was young and we called him Sambo. That was the only big cat Brian ever interacted with.

One thing we could all bond over was racehorses. Dad was still wearing the same red plaid shirt he'd had on when he won a horse race back in the eighties. He wasn't so involved anymore, but he still had one room of his house filled with all the trophies, saddles, and blankets he won in the racing business.

Me and Brian went to just about every horse race Dad was in. One big race I will never forget was the Triple Crown in Bandera, Texas. We took a horse named Amelio Jet. I got the job of walking her to the paddock, but keep in mind now, Dad always thought it was cool to get his horses to rear up on their hind legs. It's funny how he made me walk that horse when he knew I was scared of them rearing up like that. Well, Amelio Jet did that halfway to the paddock, pulled the rope out of my hands, and off she went running up this huge hill and back before Dad caught her.

I just knew he was gonna kill me because the horse would be too tired now to run that race. But he took her on to the paddock and then the starting gate. Well, off they go and with God and Lady Luck on my side, she won by half a link and Dad was the proudest man alive. He won the Texas Triple Crown with a horse he raised and trained.

In 2000, Brian became even sicker. He was no longer talking or eating, just waiting to die. Hospice had to come care for him at the house while I worked in the zoo, just to come home every hour to see the person I loved lying on the sofa bed in the living room looking at the ceiling.

It sounds terrible to say this, but while I'd be at work, I'd pray Brian would die, for God to end his pain. But it didn't happen fast. We continued to have him treated and it went up and down with his T-cell count and by the time it was undetectable, the treatments had already ruined his liver and kidneys.

One night just days before Christmas, his pain was so bad I called for an ambulance to take him to Norman Regional Hospital. He was down to nothing, mentally and physically.

The doctors in the ER treated me like I had just brought in my dog to be put to sleep. There was nothing much they could do other than give him a big shot of morphine, which they informed me would kill him. I couldn't even believe what was coming out of their mouths. The man was in so much pain he'd quit talking days prior, so it was up to me. "Give him the shot," I said, "and may God forgive me if it kills him."

Brian lived through the night. The next day he was to be discharged back into my care.

We wheeled him out of the emergency room to the car, I picked him up to put him in the seat, and I felt him take his last breath. My husband died in my arms. It was just a few days before Christmas: December 21, 2001.

Since he died outside, they would not let me bring him back in the hospital. I sat in the car with him, a sheet over his body, until the funeral home came and got him. It was one of the worst things I've ever been through, sitting in that parking lot with my dead husband, with no one to give us any compassion or dignity.

The funeral was held at the zoo; the first real funeral we had on the grounds. I was so mad when Brian died, I wanted to go to the cemetery and dig him up and beat his ass for leaving me here alone. But then I'd remember the last year of his life, watching him lie there sick, getting so thin you wouldn't even know him. Grief hits you in so many different ways.

A lot of gay men died horrible, lonely deaths during the AIDS crisis and their stories died with them. From what I hear, Netflix never mentioned Brian, which is a real shame because erasing the history of AIDS has gone on too long. Now with this book, I know the love Brian and I had for each other will survive on this earth, long after I've joined him in Heaven. Our relationship was far from perfect, but I made good on my commitment: "till death do us part."

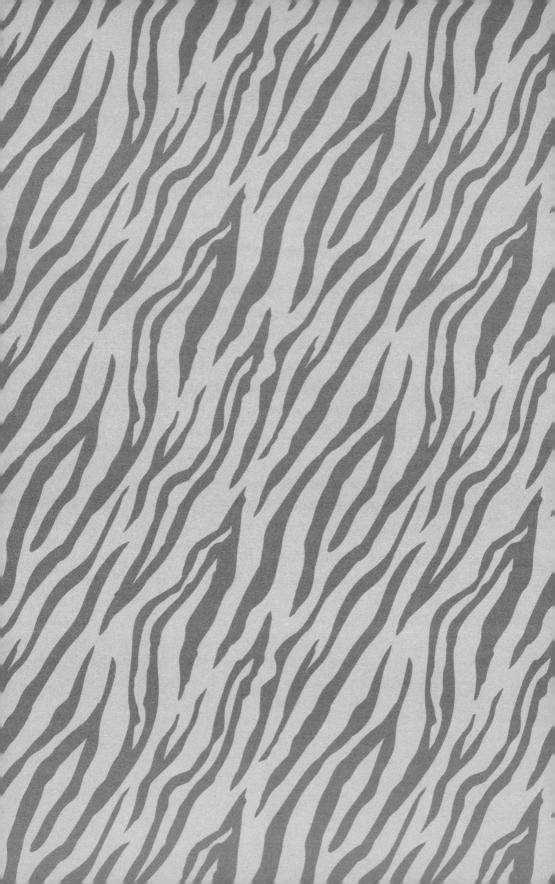

# PART TWO

# HERO IN THE WILDERNESS

# CHAPTER 8

Before Brian died, he'd been tailgating outside Heaven's door for a good year. I'd had time to process, and in many ways it was a relief when his pain finally ended. I'd been through a lot of trials and tribulations in my life, but now I was determined to start fresh and clean, and to avoid drug addicts at all costs.

Then I met one of the world's worst scumbags, JC Hartpence, and naturally my dumb ass fell right in love with him. At the time he was so good-looking, and smart. My mom hated him—she never told me that but I could tell. It wasn't because he was gay; Mom had become close with Brian, and mourned his death with me. But there was something she didn't like about JC.

Mom had good intuition, even though I never would've admitted it to her. JC was an abusive drunk, and addicted to hydrocodone. He was mean as hell but I had no self-esteem at all so I guess I thought I deserved it. Whenever he'd beat on me I never hit him back; I felt sorry for him. He was sick in the head, just like my dad had been.

I was really aching to get out in the world and do some traveling. It'd been a long time since I'd done something fun, what with taking care of the park and my sick husband. I had a lot of mouths to feed. And that's when I came up with this idea to start doing road shows with the animals.

Doing shows on the road seemed like an ideal way to keep the memorial park funded and functioning, and also a good way to avoid my abusive relationship.

We hired a manager for the zoo to help Mom look after everything, and I focused on getting bookings. Someone had donated a 1969 Frito-Lay delivery truck to the zoo; it was old and busted and ugly as hell, but I figured it could do what I needed it to. I'd pack up a few of the animals and some stage equipment and go to schools, church camps, town fairs, wherever they'd have us, and try to teach people about exotic animal habitats and the importance of protecting our environment. Most of the time our audiences were children, and they all had a hard time pronouncing my name, Joe Schreibvogel. They'd call me "Exotic Joe" instead. That turned into Joe Exotic, and that's how I got my name. I never had it legally changed because it took so much paperwork and red tape to do that, but I went by Joe Exotic from then on. Mom and Dad never really commented on it, but Dad wore every piece of merchandise I ever had that said *Joe Exotic* on it.

One of the first big road shows I did was the National Sand Bass Festival in Madill, Oklahoma, where they booked us to open for country music superstars Trick Pony. Show business had never even occurred to me before, and now I got to meet one of the biggest bands out there, and they all took pictures with me and the baby bears and tigers.

It was so inspiring, it made me want to add live music during my own shows. I bought a sound system and packed it into the Frito-Lay truck, then hired the best singer I could find, a twelve-year-old girl named Ashley Wheeler, and she sang like nobody's business. She'd sing during some curtain changes, and at halftime I'd come out and we'd sing together, mostly kid versions of rock songs, like "Lonely Road of Faith," by Kid Rock. If our shows were too far away for Ashley and her parents to travel, I'd do all the singing myself. I'd sung in high school but I never thought I'd do it professionally, and I definitely had no idea I'd one day make my own music.

I'd really gotten bitten by the showbiz bug, and was trying to find new ways to incorporate exciting elements into my shows. I even started attending meetings for a Magic Club in Oklahoma City. What I wanted were some easy magic tricks I could do, but I ended up meeting a kid named JP Wilson, and his dad, Paul Wilson. JP was only about twelve, but he was the best magician in the club, and Paul was a great guy, and a well-known salesman at a major car dealership in Oklahoma City. Me and Paul got to be good friends, and he and JP started coming on the road with me.

The magic shows started out with just some simple little tricks to get kids' attention, like making a rod go through a balloon, pulling a dove out of a hat, or making a rabbit disappear. Mostly JP would do them in front of the curtain while I changed the scenes and got the animals ready for the next portion of the show. At the end, we did what I called a Tiger Promise, but as the show grew bigger and got longer, the tiger cubs got too tired and cranky to do the promise, so we replaced them with Little Ricky, a spider monkey.

Ricky was a real ham. Kids loved him. At the end of the show, I'd have all the kids hold their arms out in a circle, like the eco-system, and I'd translate into the microphone the promise Little Ricky wanted the kids to make to him:

> *I promise*
> *To grow up and stay healthy*
> *I will not drink and drive*
> *I will say no to drugs*
> *And I won't pick on anyone else*
> *Because of the way they look or talk*

To this day, I get letters from people who made that promise to Little Ricky. If they were making promises to me, I doubt they'd have remembered all these years later, but people feel powerfully connected to animals in a way that stays with them forever. These shows meant so much to me, and really brought joy and happiness into people's lives.

JP and Ashley—and Little Ricky—grew up with the show, but the fact is that those kids taught me as much as I ever taught them, and I had all the respect in the world for them. Just because we are older doesn't mean we are wiser all the time. They taught me how to have faith, and how to believe in myself and others. Standing on stage with all those people clapping and having fun gave me the energy I needed to feel good about myself.

Our little show had grown into a two-hour theatrical event, with magic, singing, and exotic animals. Big-time things were happening, so I was able to buy a 2001 Chevy club cab pickup and a thirty-foot race car trailer to pull behind it, with a living quarter in the front. We were booking theaters and malls in Oklahoma, Texas, and Nebraska, and we even did some shows in Kansas City, Missouri.

But between all that and the zoo, we also needed to hire more help. That was when I first met John Finlay.

Finlay was living in nearby Pauls Valley at the time, with his girlfriend. He came to work for me and went on the road with us to Dodge City, Kansas, and then to Emporia, Kansas, on the way back. He liked to drive, which was great for me; I got to relax a bit in the passenger seat. As we drove those long distances we got to talking, and got to knowing each other real well.

A couple nights after we got back, I got a phone call to come save him, and found him outside his apartment, screaming his head off while this fat chick was throwing shit off his balcony. What a mess he was. Nineteen years old, living with a girl that had to weigh three hundred–plus pounds. I told him he could stay with JC and me, and set him up on my living room couch until he could get himself situated.

I always felt bad for Finlay because he really did have a lot of talent, but no one ever believed in him. He didn't have much of a chance with his upbringing. He grew up with the worst kind of hoarder, piles of bottles, jugs, other people's trash just everywhere. You had to walk sideways through the house and follow tunnels through the trash and crap to get to his bedroom, where he slept on a bare mattress on the floor. That's the home he grew up in.

Let me tell you, that boy's mother should have her ass kicked for raising someone with no responsibilities. All that said, I was glad to have Finlay around. We got along great—he was starting to come around and loosen up—and yes, I had a crush on him, but I wasn't thinking anything romantic. I had JC living with me, but

JC's drunk ass was getting increasingly pissed off at how much I was smiling now that I had a friend in Finlay.

Finally I'd had enough of JC and his smacking me around. Maybe Finlay's presence made me feel emboldened. I sat JC down and told him I wanted him to leave, and gave him a couple weeks to get his shit together and get out.

That night as I slept I heard a click, and woke up to a .45 semi-auto pointed at my forehead. JC was falling-over drunk, crying, and dangerously waving that gun around. I didn't move but yelled for Finlay to get out of the house.

There I sat on the edge of the bed, the barrel of a gun smacking me in my forehead and mouth, wondering if JC was sick enough to really do it. Finlay had called 911, so highway patrol and the sheriff's office were all sitting outside. Five and a half hours later, JC finally passed out and the police were able to get in and arrest him. That was the last time I ever saw him. I refused to bail him out; it was the only way I could think to break away from that relationship. He spent thirty days in jail and got out and went back to Kansas, where he committed terrible, terrible crimes, and is now serving life in prison for murder.

Soon after JC was gone, Finlay and I became a thing. And I have to give him credit, because he worked his ass off for that zoo, and working hard was not something that came naturally to him. Every cage that was built from the day he started was built by us, together. Finlay spent countless hours welding, as well as driving around to rescue animals. And that man could butcher a cow in five minutes flat to feed the tigers. He was amazing working with Brutus, a big tiger we had in the yard.

Finlay also knew how to do pyrotechnics, which we started

adding into our stage show. Before we got the fancy pyro boards, we mixed it ourselves, with the pods running on car remotes to set them off. Once in Odessa, Texas, Finlay was walking on the stage with the pods and one of them blew up. Turned out someone's car had the same remote code as the one we were using to set off the pyrotechnics. When they unlocked their car in the parking lot, it triggered ours and the pod blew up in Finlay's face, burning him so bad they had to fly him to Abilene, Texas, to the burn center.

Did that stop the show? No. No matter what anyone says about Finlay, he was committed to our cause, and we put on a hell of an entertaining presentation.

The two of us got Prince Alberts together while we were on tour in Kansas. We just got a wild hair one night and went and got them done. This lady used a McDonald's straw for a catheter and a fingernail file. We had no idea what we were doing, but it damn sure wasn't on the up-and-up. Took about three days for the bleeding to stop, and Finlay had to go to the ER. Why would someone do something like that? you might ask, and I don't have a good answer for you. But I did like having it. It was like a secret, until it wasn't. Then it became a highlight.

It wasn't long after that we were doing a show in Lansing, Michigan, at a mall, and a young man named Paul Rowe applied for a job with the show.

Paul was about five foot ten with black hair and a nice body, slim build, and very good-looking. I never even dreamed of being with two people at the same time, but it was about a week down the road after he came to work for me that Paul, John Finlay, and me—we all just clicked.

It worked out pretty well. Finlay and Paul were both into the

Insane Clown Posse and playing PlayStation all night long. And like always I was all about work, nonstop, all day, but I liked to go do things after our shows, red-carpet events, and generally be sociable. Finlay hated all that stuff, but Paul liked it. It all just fell into place; none of us forced it.

Between the two of them, I felt like I got enough love to get me through the day. Everything I did was equal: if I spent $500 on one, I did on the other. They both had a Mustang, their own PlayStation, and their own TV in the bedroom of the tour bus.

Yeah, I know where your mind goes, but it was not about the sex. It was about one of us always having a friend and someone to do things with. Of course I can see now that I just always felt like it was my job to fix these truly broken men, and the only way I knew how to do it was to love them with everything I had. Neither Finlay nor Paul Rowe was ever great to me, but there was love between us. We took care of each other, each in our own unique way. Maybe it wasn't perfect, maybe it was far from normal, but it worked for me at the time.

# CHAPTER 9

**B**ack when I still had the store in Texas, I used to help out at a wilderness park in Oklahoma a few days a week. They had three chimps there: Joe, Lilly, and Coco. The chimps had a nice enclosure but they were miserable. The owners kept robbing Lilly of her babies and selling them for tens of thousands of dollars. While I was there, Lilly had a stillborn baby that they couldn't get away from her. She hung on to it so long it rotted in her hands.

I never really had time to sit and spend with Lilly because the place was so big and there was so much to do. But to this day I think about the look in her eyes when she was holding on to that dead baby.

Years later, I got a call from Steve Martin (the animal trainer, not the actor) in California, wanting to know if I would take three chimps and a grizzly bear. He'd bought these chimps as breeders and found out they were too old to breed. Turned out they were my old friends Joe, Lilly, and Coco. Joe had a white pigment in his right eye that made him easy to identify. I was so happy to know

I'd have a chance to help these three out. Mom and Dad built our primate house and we took them in.

Getting to know these chimps changed my life, and changed my relationship with animals. I'd sit outside their cage with Lilly and eat breakfast, lunch, and dinner with her. We colored in coloring books, drank Cokes, and even smoked a cig together once in a while. She loved to play in a mirror while I put lipstick on her. But mostly we would sit together and just look into each other's eyes. She told me her whole life story through her eyes, about being in cages all the time with nothing to do, having to make good out of pulling grass and placing little pebbles in circles around her, and the heartache of missing her babies that people stole from her. Lilly was always a sullen girl; she was brokenhearted.

Is there a God? Who knows. The Indians believe in the spirit; they cherish the dirt, the trees, and every animal, because it's about the soul and the spirit of each thing, not about who or what it is. Looking into the eyes of an orangutan, or a chimp, there is something there that we are missing. They lock eyes with you and it's like they become part of you for just a split-second. Until you open up your heart and soul to the spirit of what animals are, you will never experience it for real. It was like Lilly's soul was telling me the story of how we all got here, and what we are all supposed to do to help each other.

They are us, we were them, we are the same. I do in fact believe we all evolved from animals, and apes are our ancestors, and when you look deep into the eyes of an ape you can see the story being told, without a word being spoken.

I think that is why I got along so well with my tigers and my chimps: they can look right into your soul. They read your soul. I could walk any person looking for a job down Tiger Alley and the tigers would let me know if they were a good person or not.

I needed to make sure my chimps were comfortable, which meant we needed to step up our employee situation at the park. There were never any "volunteers" working on my property because I'm not one for babysitting. I set up a trailer park in the zoo for the employees to live in who didn't have anywhere else to go.

That trailer park was the biggest problem I had at the zoo. It didn't matter who I hired—married couples or single people—it was a constant fuck fest. And these people, they had no taste whatsoever. I bet that zoo is responsible for at least seven babies being born into this world, and all by people who had no concern about the future.

My relationship may have seemed like a lot, but it was nothing compared to my staff. If there wasn't a cop at the trailers where they lived, there was an ambulance, because they were drunk and fighting. I got the blame for everything, and they always had me in the middle of drama. Once in Michigan, I finished a show and an elderly woman came up to the stage and asked, "Are you Joe Exotic?"

I said, "Yes, that is what the big sign above the stage says."

She said, "You're paying for my daughter to get an abortion."

I was like, "Ma'am, you are *so* barking up the wrong tree because I need Benadryl just looking at women's tits, I am so gay."

She said her daughter worked at the zoo, and it was my fault they all slept together. I let her know I was not her daughter's babysitter, nor was I responsible for how a grown woman behaves when the zoo is closed, and that was the end of that.

One of the only people who ever really gave a shit about coming to work and keeping the zoo running professionally was John

Reinke. The bionic man with no legs. Here is a man for you—this guy worked circles around the two-legged people at the zoo and they cared enough about him to stand by and watch him work his ass off before they would lift a finger to help him.

Rink—that's what we called him—first came to the zoo as a customer and sponsored a grizzly bear named Ozzy. But it was a lion named Bonedigger that Rink really fell in love with. Bonedigger was disabled but he was a lot of fun, and he had four wiener dogs as his best friends. It was adorable. Rink ended up moving to the zoo and became the manager for fourteen years. We were like brothers; we worked good together, and I had a lot of respect for him and the work he put in. He ran the crews and took care of all the paperwork, and really kept everything in top shape while I was out on the road. He bent over backward for the zoo, my parents and me, and those animals.

Most of the people who worked for me thought I was a major asshole because we worked until the animals were taken care of, even if that meant eighteen-hour days. People may think I overworked my employees, but damn it, these animals could not care for themselves because they were in cages depending on us.

No one was forced to stay working there; everyone could have walked whenever they wanted, but to hear them talk for TV, I'm a devil who worked them so hard for nothing, like they were chained up or some shit. They stayed because they got to work with the most amazing beasts on our planet and it gave them the ability to brag to their friends, not to mention they got paid. Considering the drunken messes I had to put up with, they were basically unemployable anywhere else. Large portions of my time were spent just trying to keep them clean.

There were a few other die-hard workers who were really there for the animals and gave up a lot of their lives to come help. Two that come to mind are Ben and Satrina McAnally. Ben had the ability to work with tigers like I did, and he worked his ass off, while Satrina did the books and the office work and took care of the babies. I remember Satrina saying, "I got the most depressing job at this zoo sitting here every day looking at the checkbook in the hole." People thought our lives were all sparkles and hundred-dollar bills until they realized we were always working.

As the touring show grew, we were traveling the entire United States, booked forty-two weeks a year. Our caravan included eleven staff members in a bus, with two semis following with all the props, cages, and animals in them. The show was a full two-and-half-hour magic show and animal display, complete with pyrotechnics and illusions like you would see in Vegas. The largest crowd we ever had was in Eagle Pass, Texas, to a mostly Spanish audience. Just like Selena did a crossover tour, so did I. The show runners taught me to say enough Spanish to perform and communicate with the crowd, which was so big, there were people as far as my eyes could see.

I did a show for a monkey convention, with an organization called UAPPEAL (Uniting a Politically Proactive Exotic Animal League), in Hot Springs, Arkansas. They hired me to come do the magic show for entertainment. I wasn't sure what to expect; I had monkeys at the zoo but I was pretty adamantly against private ownership of animals like that. My monkeys were too mean to be brought out to socialize with strangers.

A private owner has exotic animals for pets, and pays to care for them all by themselves. I'd really only dealt with private owners when I was handling rescues, so I'd only known of bad situations. Before that, I hadn't realized that being a responsible pet owner was a lot like being a responsible parent: don't do it if you can't afford it. These monkey people—they loved their monkeys just as much as people love their children. And when I say they loved them, I mean they treated them like family members. *Expensive* family members. Hell, some of these monkeys had full bedrooms like a child, and outside playgrounds in huge enclosures. No cages involved.

This one lady Barbara had a huge macaque—I mean this thing was at least ninety pounds, and it sat at the hotel dinner table with glassware and dishes, not paper plates, and it didn't touch a thing until Barbara said it was okay to eat. Then it ate with a fork and spoon, better than a young child, and drank out of a glass. I was flabbergasted.

These private owners were really no different from me. In fact, if I'm being honest, their animals were better off than mine. At the zoo, we had to make a profit to keep it going, whereas these private owners treated their animals better than most people treat their own kids.

At that point I started to have more of an open mind about supporting responsible exotic animal ownership. If you can afford a monkey and keep him happy and healthy, by no means do I have the right to say you can't. I learned a lot from that convention, es- pecially about how animal rights organizations will twist the truth to try to make private owners look bad. Groups like PETA and the HSUS were always giving monkey owners a hard time.

People who are never around animals couldn't possibly under- stand what these creatures do to your heart and soul. You will find that people who grew up in the country are far more understanding than city folk who have never experienced finding an injured animal and nursing it back to health, or raising a goat, sheep, or cow from birth and seeing it as a family member and not just an animal.

When we had the pet store I never knew anything about the underbelly of exotic animal ownership. We always kept to ourselves back then. But now, after hearing these monkey owners' stories about their fights with the government regarding the legality of their pets, I wanted to know more. Something about it didn't seem right. Who is Uncle Sam to tell me what kind of animal I'm allowed to own, let alone some mysterious nonprofit swooping in and telling me what to do.

With all the things I did in my life, all the mistakes I'd made along the way, this was hands down the biggest one. My desire to stick up for the little guy led me to start asking too many questions. I put myself on the radar of the wrong people, and worse, I started pissing them off. What I was really doing was putting a huge target on my back.

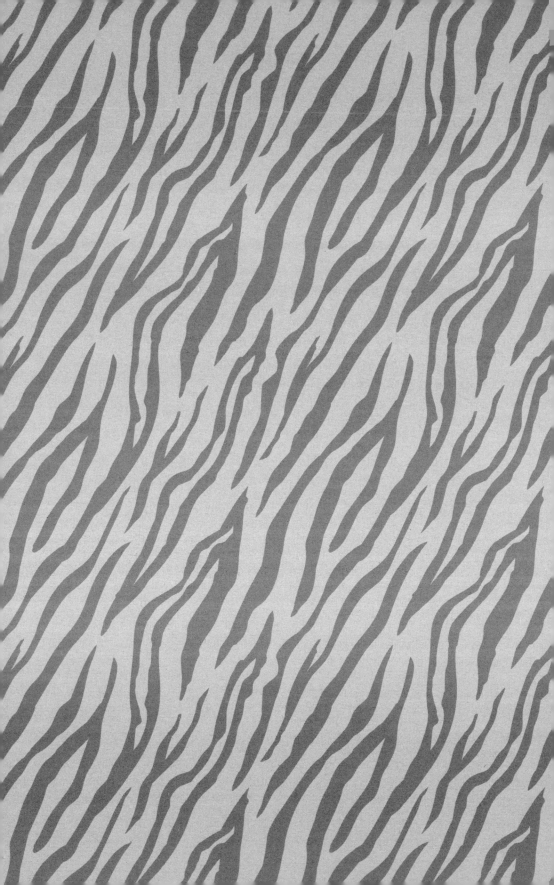

# CHAPTER 10

A lot of people think all big cats can be cared for the same, and that is not true.

Tigers like the snow; lions do not.

Tigers love the water and swimming; lions hate it.

Tigers can be tamer and more trustworthy; lions are unpredictable and way more possessive of their food and toys.

Tigers are jumpers; lions are not. That means tigers climb fences more than lions do, so tiger cages have to be covered, or constructed much higher than an ordinary cage.

Then there are leopards: also jumpers and far more dangerous. When one turns on you or gets mean, they go right for your throat. Tigers will most of the time bite and let go, or rip an arm off and leave. A lion will lie on you like it is protecting its food while it punishes you beyond belief. If a lion were to get ahold of someone at my park, the most humane thing for me to do would be to shoot that person in the head to put them out of their misery, so they don't die from being mauled to death. Never had to do it, thank God, but it's a scenario that would keep me up at night sometimes.

The same way I believe humans evolved from monkeys, I believe all species of cats evolved from a common ancestor: the saber-toothed tiger. It's my belief that during the Ice Age, saber-toothed tigers got trapped on different continents, and over time they adapted to their environment and became what we know as lions and various species of tigers.

Despite their many differences, I had a strong belief that I could get a tiger and a lion to mate successfully. Many people had tried to breed them but it never worked, because they killed each other. However, my saber-toothed tiger theory would seem to suggest breeding was possible.

I started by putting a baby male lion and a female tiger in an enclosure, and letting them grow up together. That way, there was no discrimination. They were unaware there were any differences between them.

When this nondiscriminatory lion and this nondiscriminatory tiger reached sexual maturity (at about the age of five), they bred, and had four cubs. These cubs are called ligers.

Experts had told me that these ligers would be sterile, which would mean the experiment was over. But they were wrong: the males were sterile, but the females were not.

A lot of people were intrigued with the research I was doing. Keep in mind, most people are all about money, so they never took the time and expense to do this the way I did. But I was lucky enough to have all these cubs at the same age. I had the means, desire, and know-how to keep my research going. I raised a male lion cub with a female liger, and I raised a white tiger with another female liger. Then, five years down the road, I was the first in the world to produce a natural-bred and -born litter of liligers and taligers.

Crossbred cats are born without a growth-limiting gene, so they grow their entire lives. At two years old, the male liliger stood twelve feet eight inches tall. He was the same tan color as a lion, with rosettes and spots on his head.

The taliger was just as big. He came out yellow, with big rosettes on his body and spots on his head.

When I announced that I had the first set of taligers ever born, a couple of scientists from Texas A&M contacted me. They were working with the National Institutes of Health, doing research on hybrids. I sent them blood and tissue samples from my cats, which were then written about in some academic papers. It was their belief that due to their increased size, hybrids will be the only ones to survive the climate change of the next hundred years. It is a belief I share.

Now that I had a third generation of crossbreeds, scientists came to the zoo one day and we removed one testicle from a male taliger, and one from a male liger, and found there to be live sperm, just not enough to produce babies. We needed to crossbreed a fourth time, to get the males to no longer be sterile. I bred a liliger female cub back with a male lion again and produced the world's first L3 liger. I also produced a litter with the female liliger and a white male tiger: the world's first pure-white L3 taliger.

The more we crossbred, the bigger and tamer they got. I worked with some of the country's top geneticists on the genetics of big cats. I was on a roll, making history and showing the world that cats are all genetically the same and can breed as long as they grow up together. I wanted to keep reversing evolution until I could get the exact look of a saber-toothed tiger, which looked more like a lion to begin with.

Since my study began, people are now breeding house cats with exotic cats, lions with leopards, and so on. We have now proved that they are genetically the same.

Breeding tigers has gotten me in a lot of trouble over the years. Animal rights groups say it's cruel to pull an animal from its mother when it's born. Problem is, in captivity it is stupid and dangerous to let a mama raise a cub. Oftentimes a cub will end up being killed by its mother or father. And even if it survives, without human contact from the very beginning it can grow up to be a human-killer, which means it's more likely to be put down.

At birth, I would take cubs away from their mom before their eyes opened. When working with or feeding them, I'd chuff and blow in their mouths so the scent of me was what they registered. Tigers register a smell for life. When their eyes opened ten to twelve days after birth, I'd be the first thing they saw, which caused them to imprint on me. This allowed me to raise them as if I were one of them instead of just an owner or trainer. We were a family.

If you see photos of me with my animals, I was always blowing in their mouths and kissing them because that is what assures them everything is okay. That is why I got away with loving on so many full-grown tigers all the time. Levi, a male liger; Baco, a male liliger; and Itsy, a female liliger were the ones I worked and bonded with the most.

Regardless of what anyone thinks about me and my work, I had a valid license in good standing with the United States Department of Agriculture Animal and Plant Health Inspection Service

(USDA APHIS), and they had their veterinary inspectors come to my zoo about every three months to make sure I had proper protocols in place and the animals were cared for. I had over seventy species of animals at the zoo, and every time I got a new animal in, I had to have the protocols for the USDA to prove I had done my research and knew how to care for them. Their diet, their environment, and their enrichment needs were all regulated upon getting any new animal.

The hardest to learn how to care for were these Canadian beavers we got in. We made a large indoor pool area and built them this badass wooden house that was half in the water and half out, just like a beaver dam would be. We put willow trees and such in there so they'd have wood and bark to chew on, along with their main diet that was specially made for beavers.

Right after we got them all set up and moved into their exhibit, guess what they did: they ate the entire house, in one night, and chewed up the landscape post.

I guess you could say that was one time we all had a brain fart, since we built a beaver house out of wood. Some things you learn the hard way.

Here are some of my favorite types of animals I've had:

- **Hamsters/gerbils:** Every one of these little bastards I ever had bit me. I could walk in with twenty full-grown tigers and never get hurt but pick up a hamster and bleed every time. Still, I always loved having them around.
- **Pigeons:** Very cool creatures, but they do shit all over everything. I ended up with over five hundred of them at one time.

- **Guinea pigs:** Cute, tame, never bite, but they stink if you don't clean their cage often enough, and they love to play at night when you're sleeping.
- **Ducks, turkeys, peacocks:** I had so many of all these, and the people who came to the zoo loved getting photos taken with the peacocks and turkeys.
- **Barn owls:** Very cool, very sharp claws. They can be taught to fly to you.
- **North American porcupines:** Caught my first one in Wyoming and then had some at the zoo. I made Indian-style jewelry with the quills they shed.
- **African crested porcupines:** These are so awesome, tame enough to walk on a leash. They have quills larger than pencils. We'd use them as toothpicks and ink pens.
- **Opossums:** Fun little animals, cross-eyed almost all the time. They slobber a lot. During the spring, if you see one that's been hit on the road, stop and check—in the pouch there might be live babies to save.
- **Squirrels:** I had ground squirrels and tree squirrels. The tree ones make better pets and can be tamed more easily. Here at the prison, guys sit outside and have the squirrels so tame they'll come sit in your lap.
- **Raccoons:** I love raccoons. They tend to get grumpy when they eat.
- **Skunks:** Skunks make the best pets: they don't make any noise, they use a litter box, and they play just like a dog or cat. They're easy to de-scent. All you do is remove the anal glands. Don't even have to do surgery for that.

Those were my favorites, but I wanted to provide you with a list of every kind of animal I ever had. My memory is photographic so it should be pretty exhaustive:

| | | |
|---|---|---|
| 4-horn sheep | Foxes | Scottish Highland |
| Aardvarks | Goats | cattle |
| Alligators | Grizzly bears | Servals |
| Badgers | Iguanas | Snakes (sixty-eight |
| Bats | Jackals | different venomous |
| Beavers | Leopards | ones) |
| Black bears | Ligers | Sphynx cats |
| Bobcats | Liligers | Spider monkeys |
| Buffalo | Lions | Squirrel monkeys |
| Caimans | Lynx | Taligers |
| Camels | Macaques | Tigers |
| Capuchin monkeys | Mona monkeys | Tigons |
| Chimps | Ostriches | White lions |
| Cattle | Parrots | White tigers |
| Coyotes | Pigs | White-faced capuchins |
| Crocodiles | Poison dart frogs | White-tailed deer |
| Emus | Rabbits | Wolves |
| Eurasian eagle-owls | Red deer | Zebras |
| Ferrets | Saltwater fish | Zebus |
| Fishing cats | | |

Oh, and of course dogs, including dachshunds, blue heelers, rotties, standard and toy poodles, cocker spaniels, Australian shepherds, German shepherds, Dobermans, toy Manchesters, and mutts out the ass.

# CHAPTER 11

I'd first heard of Carole Baskin back in about 2006. I'd picked up an Oklahoma City newspaper and on the front page was a story about this little, shitty, nasty roadside zoo in Oklahoma. The more I read, I realized it was about me and my zoo.

I was proud of the work I was doing. I had a successful entertainment company, I was performing cutting-edge genetic research, and I was rescuing and housing some of the most amazing creatures on God's green earth, all in the name of my good brother GW. So, who the fuck was this Carole Baskin—I had no idea who she was—who claimed in this article to be a reporter, even though, to my knowledge, she had never even been to my zoo when she "reported" this story about me?

Aw, man, it really pissed me off to see this woman making up these stories about my park. But I didn't fully comprehend at the time what a predicament I'd gotten myself into once Carole had set her sights on me.

Now, I'd had my run-ins with PETA before—long before. When

we were out on the road, we'd do petting shows, sometimes with adult tigers and sometimes with babies. Like for the Old Paris Flea Market in OKC, we'd take a young tiger down to the Habana Inn and let people come up and pet it, and all this was done to promote attendance at the flea market. PETA hated me doing these kinds of petting shows. And let me tell you, God help you if you get on the wrong side of PETA, because they have the money to stay on your ass, either through lawsuits or making videos and online campaigns about you. It never ends.

As much as those fuckers drove me nuts, at least with PETA they don't pick and choose their targets. PETA hates everyone in the animal industry; not like this hypocrite Carole Baskin. So I looked her up to see what she was all about. As a former police chief, I've never quite let go of the investigative habit. That is when I found the *People* magazine article called "Too Purrfect": it appeared that this man Don Lewis was missing, and the article said his kids speculated Carole Baskin may have put him through the meat grinder and fed him to tigers.

You'd think something in me would have said, *This woman seems to have little regard for life, maybe don't keep digging into her past.* But no, I kept right on it, because once I started I was truly shocked by what I found out. Let me tell you about Carole Baskin.

Carole's a short lady with dirty-blond hair, and she kind of looks like one of those people whose breath you can taste when you're near them. Back in 2003, just a couple years after I'd opened my park, Carole incorporated Big Cat Rescue, a so-called sanctuary down in Tampa, Florida. It looked to me like she was doing ten times more animal exploitation than I ever did. She sold every kind of tour: kids' camps, work tours, feeding tours, keeper tours.

She even used to have people renting cabins overnight with full-grown mountain lions in them. And of course she used to breed cats—same as the rest of us in the industry.

On top of the outright hypocrisy, Carole had a memorial list of animals that died in her care that was shocking—*shocking*—to see. Big Cat Rescue has on average eleven to fifteen tigers and lions at their place at one time, to keep the overhead low and the profit line high. If you go to her Facebook page and website, you'll see there's always one dying or very sick and in need of donations. When I started tallying it up, it was like eighty-four, and by the time I gave up counting, she was up to 226 dead big cats.

The causes of death she listed were things like "euthanized for unknown pain conditions," "choked on straw," "ate leaves," "dead in cage," "cancer"—oh my God, the number of cats there that died of cancer was crazy—and the second-highest cause of death was kidney failure. I had over 260 tigers and lions at one time, and never, not one time, did one die from kidney failure or cancer.

Come to find out, her property used to be a junkyard, and the water source she pumped in the cages was from a pond I think still may have all the junk cars and batteries in it. I had county records that showed it was a junkyard, and I interviewed her staff that had been there to help build the park, and they concurred. They had filled the junkyard with water and turned it into a pond and lagoon.

The seemingly contaminated water was being pumped into the cages with no filter, run through every cage and back into the pond, and you know if the junk is still in there, the water quality is bad from the metal and batteries.

This Carole Baskin, with all these dead cats, thinks she should be able to tell other people how to run their business. She claims to be an expert, but she doesn't know shit.

She tells the public that crossbred tigers are too big for moms to birth, or they are born dead or deformed, all kinds of stuff. From what I have been told, Carole has never been around a tiger giving birth. I bred more hybrids than anyone in the world (except maybe some Russians), and out of the over 150 hybrids I produced, never was there a birth defect or a stillborn baby or a birth complication. The babies are no bigger at birth than those of a purebred tiger or lion, even though they later grow to be much bigger. At my park, it was all done naturally, with no artificial breeding or anything, and this scared Carole so bad that she had to paint me as Frankenstein to the public to try to discredit me.

How does a woman like Carole claim to be an expert on big cats when, to my knowledge, she has never personally bred a litter of tigers or lions in her life? You would think that as an expert she would have hands-on training and experience in order to even weigh in with an opinion. I call bullshit on everything she claims about breeding, bottle-feeding, or anything else related to big cats.

Another one of Carole's often-repeated misstatements is that white tigers are inbred to be white. That's not true. The white gene is natural in the wild, carried by an orange Bengal tiger. You can tell because they have green eyes, not orange eyes, and you cannot make them have white babies; only God controls that. You can breed two white tigers together and never get a white baby—it just depends on how strong that gene is carried in that animal.

In the 1960s President Eisenhower received, as a gift, the last white tiger cub captured in the wild. Only a couple years ago were new white tigers spotted in the wild. And yet, despite Carole's claims on inbreeding, there has only been one white tiger in the world known to be born with a facial defect. His name was Kenny, and he lived at Turpentine Creek Wildlife Refuge in Arkansas. Kenny looked like he had Down syndrome. He died years ago but they all still exploit his photo. He was the only one ever, and it was a birth defect, not a genetic defect.

Texas A&M did an awesome paper on white tiger genetics, and out of every tiger tested in America, no white tigers were related. The funny thing is, Carole donated blood from a white tiger to the project! You will never get Carole to admit that, but Big Cat Rescue is acknowledged as a DNA donor in the paper.

Carole likes to tell this story about how she went to Minnesota and bought out and shut down a fur farm. I called the owner of that fur farm, and she said by no means had Carole shut her down. She had sold Carole fifty-six bobcat babies to take back and sell as pets, which Carole did. In fact, Carole even wrote a book about how to pick an exotic cat for a pet.

The best part? There are USDA receipts showing Carole paid $95,000 for those cats she claimed to rescue. I guess she thought going to an auction, buying some animals, and pimping them out at Big Cat Rescue was somehow equal to rescuing those animals from the pet trade. The woman must drink bong water for break-fast and probably made beef jerky out of Don Lewis for lunch.

Carole had a website, 911animalabuse.com, and she started posting about me, my park, and my touring show. I had my own website created, 911animalabuse.*org*, showing proof that Carole was apparently lying about those bobcats. Most of those fifty-six baby cats died under her care. She had no idea what to do with them.

When Carole started her park, she thought she was a flower child, dressed like a lost hippie of the sixties with flowers around her head all the time. Except this was in the 1990s, and it wasn't peace and love Carole was smoking, it was hate and revenge. She apparently hated Don Lewis so much because he would not spend money on her or her daughter (although Carole supposedly hates her daughter, too). In the last line of Carole's diary, seen by yours truly, it says, "I wish there were some way out for me."

If all Carole wanted was to find "some way out" and get away from Don, she could've left whenever she wanted. But I don't think that was all she wanted; she may have wanted Don's money, too. She seemed obsessed with owning it all and couldn't lose the comfortable life she'd grown accustomed to.

I spent days and days talking to people who rode around with Don Lewis, and knew Don better than Carole. Don wanted a divorce, these people told me, and his friends thought that Carole knew Don wanted a divorce. It is my opinion that late one night, Carole and her father, Vernon, may have killed Don Lewis in his sleep by hitting him in the head with a crowbar. I strongly believe they then ground him up in a commercial meat grinder, fed what they could to the tigers, and buried the remaining parts of Don's body under a septic tank that was installed right before Carole reported Don missing. Carole denies she murdered Don, and while she has not been charged with any crime, the case remains open and Don's children have offered a reward for anyone with information into Don's death.

I think there should be enough evidence to indict her for conspiracy to commit murder even without a body. The officials have Don's will, and it says right there on page two that "this instrument was designed by Carole Lewis," and in the first sentence it says "In case of my disappearance . . ." Who the hell puts that in a will instead of "upon my death," besides crazy Carole Baskin? Everything to do with Don—and I mean everything—was left to Carole. Even voting rights in his companies. His kids got next to nothing.

Five years after he may have been fed to tigers, Carole was able to declare Don dead and collect his millions.

Carole tried to get the public to believe Don's old secretary Anne McQueen had something to do with his death. Take it from me, this is the last thing on earth that happened. Anne even won a defamation lawsuit against Carole and got a six-figure payment and a written apology from her. I believe that when Carole is guilty of something, she throws tidbits of misinformation to the public. Like the meat grinder—she's out there trying to convince people that the meat grinder I think she used to destroy Don Lewis's body is one of those small grinders that bolts onto a tabletop. But when she reported it stolen, she said it was a commercial meat grinder. For God's sake, why am I the only one who knows this shit? I would bet my life that the meat grinder is in that pond at Big Cat Rescue.

Now Carole is telling people that if someone finds Don's bones around the original house at Big Cat Rescue, it must be part of some big setup. Why would she even be worried about that?

In my honest opinion, Carole Baskin is a psychopath who is obsessed with money and control. I believe Carole gets off on my sitting here rotting in prison as much as she gets off on the victims she may have rotting in the ground. Maybe my only chance of ever getting out of here will come because Carole is so deranged, one day she won't be able to keep up with her apparent lies, and the truth will come out.

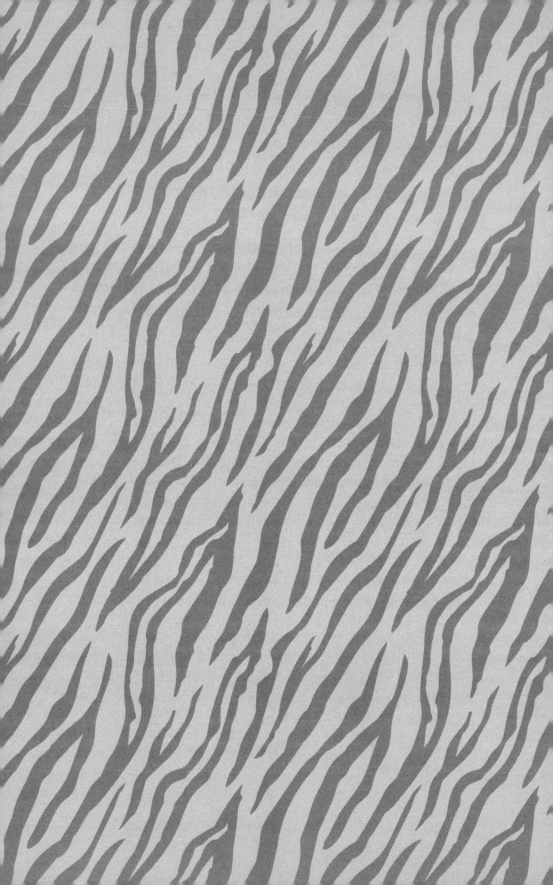

# CHAPTER 12

I've never said no to a lion or tiger that needed a home. One rescue I will never forget happened outside St. Louis, Missouri, at a sanctuary where a man had been killed. He'd left behind forty-two tigers and lions, and one leopard. We loaded up the trailers, got Rink's dad to drive an eighteen-wheeler cattle truck, and headed out to Missouri to clean this place out.

A police escort was waiting for us when we got into town, due to all the news media. They were calling me the Tiger King, and it's a name that's stuck with me ever since.

Being the Tiger King meant something to me back then. I had a duty to give a home to any tiger that needed one, and those cats in Missouri needed one. They were used to living in nothing more than dog kennels. We got them all sedated and loaded up on the truck as quickly as we could, so we could get them back to the zoo and assess the situation. Some of them had to be loaded in with a backhoe because they were so big.

One of the female tigers was very thin and sick. We put her in our medical building to care for her and the rest went to their new homes for life. In Oklahoma it is legal to doctor your own animals, but the whole time I owned the zoo I had a special relationship with our veterinarian, Dr. Green. She took great care of me and my animals. I'm sure she never expected to be treating so many exotics in her career, and since I'd had so much experience with them, I kind of taught her as much as she did me. She trusted me and Rink to do things, and we trusted her completely.

A couple weeks went by and the sick tiger was doing well enough to go out to the zoo. Keep in mind these were all strange tigers to me, but I went in with her every day while she was sick, gave her the medication, and loved on her. When it was time to move her out, I was going to save six dollars on a dart and not put her through sedation again, so I put a leash on her, a double leash, with me holding on to one side and Rink the other.

We walked her around inside the medical building. She responded just fine. The plan was to walk her outside and to her new compound. My last comment before opening the door and walking her out was, "Damn, she has big teeth."

The door opened and we made it about a foot before John Finlay spooked her and she bit down on my left leg. I hit her so she'd let go, and she did, but then she bit down again so hard her tooth broke off in my leg.

Finally she let go and grabbed on to Rink's leg, and pulled it off. It was a fake leg, remember. This whole time, Rink never let go of her. She dragged him back through the medical building right to her cage, where Rink was able to lock the door and contain her.

My blood was spraying everywhere as I just lay there bleeding out on the sidewalk. I used my belt as a tourniquet to slow the bleeding down and called 911 on my cell phone. The dispatcher at the sheriff's office answered and asked, "What is your emergency?"

I told her, "I need a helicopter and this is the last call I will be able to make because I am bleeding that bad."

She said, "Joe, is that you? Did a tiger get you?"

I said, "Yes, but don't put that over the radio." I didn't want the local law enforcement to know, or else they would make me kill the tiger.

Next thing I remember is hearing blades from the helicopter going over my head, then arriving at Norman Regional Hospital. They put drain tubes in me and stitched up most of my leg, and the doctor chose to leave the tooth in my calf muscle because he thought my body would heal around it, like it would a bullet.

I got out of the hospital to return home, except I had to leave in three days for a forty-two-week magic tour. Rink made me a square stand with a rod up my back and a seat belt to keep me in place so the stage crew could roll me around on stage. Well, I made it from Oklahoma to Dayton, Ohio, and performed there for a week, then off to Bemidji, Minnesota, where I made it two days and had to stop. My leg was so infected they took me in for emergency surgery, where they removed the tooth and scraped out my leg.

When I woke up in recovery, a nurse rattled a cup with the tooth in it and said, "Can I keep this?"

I replied, "Yes, ma'am, you may." I spent four days in the hospital and left to go back on tour. Taking a break was not an option; I needed to keep the tour going in order to fund the zoo.

The idea of traveling around in a tour bus seems stressful—wondering how the next show would go—but life was great back then. I spent nine years living in a tour bus and two semis touring the country, doing magic, teaching kids about animals, all while raising money for the zoo. I had two boyfriends, an adoring public, and more tigers than anyone in the United States.

Meeting all kinds of people on the road was amazing and scary. People got obsessed because they wanted my superpowers. I had people kiss my hands when I got done with a show and I had people follow me everywhere I went. It got to the point where I had to have a bodyguard with me on the road.

While I was dealing with all this, I found out Carole Baskin had placed me on her 911 Animal Abuse website as her "MOST WANTED." I had done my best to ignore her but the more I ignored her, the worse her seeming harassment got. She posted my entire schedule of upcoming shows. Whenever we added a new show, somehow Carole seemed to know about it. She bought a program that cost like $10,000 called Capwiz, which sent out email alerts by the thousands, all claiming I abused baby tigers.

These emails were sent to every show I did at local malls all over the country, with my magic show and cub-petting exhibits. Some malls got their inboxes jammed up with over seventy thousand emails and would ask us to leave and cancel the shows just to save their computer systems. I filed complaints with the Attorney General for clear violations of the Animal Enterprise Terrorism Act. Nothing was done.

Then it got worse. Around 2010, Carole bragged on her website she had paid someone $35,000 to follow me all over the country. This lady's name was Sue Bass, and she had stalker-level awareness of my comings and goings. And it was all reported right back to Carole. I know, I've seen the reports: through subpoenas of

Carole's emails, I've seen the communications between Sue Bass and Carole and Carole's third husband, Howard Baskin.

I guess I should say something about Howard Baskin. How to describe this man. He's older, looks like a washrag that was used for a month or so, then thrown on a countertop and left to mold. Poor Howard. I bet he has to sleep with one eye open at night, watching for the crowbar.

Howard has a law degree and it seems to me he spends his hours trolling the internet, leaving nasty comments anywhere my name is mentioned. I filed a protection order against Carole and Howard after I found out about Sue Bass, but they sent high-powered lawyers to stop me.

Through Sue Bass, Carole got so many people to believe I was an animal abuser. They would drive hours to vandalize the zoo or burn shit down, or turn up at our shows duct-taped together for sit-ins, or spray-paint graffiti on our semis, or protest outside on the streets. We had one of our employees dress up like a gorilla and stand out on the street with a sign that said, "PETA kills animals." None of the protesters wanted their picture taken with that sign in the background. That got them to go away for a while.

Why did Carole do this to me? Was it to help baby animals? No. Was she doing anything to improve the lives of my animals? No, she was making their lives worse because I had to spend all my money on her lawsuits. Carole's goal, in my mind, has never been about animals; it's been about control, and money.

This feud with Carole and Howard went on and on. They may have even had spies come in and work for us, because someone stole our mailing list. They obtained photo footage of customers on tours, and used those photos for propaganda and smear campaigns.

At one point Carole messaged Rink on Facebook and offered him $20,000 to give me up. She was trying to get him to work for her and said, "Once Joe is out of the zoo you might be able to enjoy your job." It looked to me like she'd planned on taking my zoo away from me for many years.

This is how this industry worked. Carole and others would complain there are too many tigers in America and we have to stop breeding because there are not enough sanctuaries to put them in, then a month later they are all shipping more cats in because there are none to rescue.

I know what I'm talking about. I'm the one who sold, donated, and traded baby and young tigers to nearly every so-called sanctuary in this country. They'd claim they just rescued it from a breeder, or its mom died, and then they had at least three months to let people play with it and donate money. I have no problem admitting the wrongs I've done. I kept animals in cages for money, just like Carole and the rest have. What did we all say? *A private owner abused this animal, and we need money to take care of it for the rest of its life.* You wouldn't believe how many sanctuaries in this country bought baby tigers from me so they could raise money off of saying they rescued this baby tiger from a petting zoo or a private owner.

That is the scam in the industry: using injured animals to pull on heartstrings, just like the ASPCA and HSUS commercials on TV seem to do. There's a reason the ASPCA puts on a sad Sarah McLachlan song and shows you pictures of hurt animals and then asks you for money. There's a reason you put the most crippled and sick animals up front at the zoo. It works. People will throw all their money at you if they can only help those poor animals.

Don't you ever stop to think why the cameramen are taking pictures of the hurt animals, rather than helping them? You know why. Money. They set up cameras while a dog is in mud freezing its ass off. If they really cared and didn't stage that whole scene, they would be filming themselves running in there to save the dog, not taking the time to set up professional cameras while the dog or cat suffers another minute. If a dog saw someone coming to get it out of the mud, it would be jumping on the fence saying, *Pet me, pet me*; or if it was scared of people, it would be running away to hide, not staring into a camera saying, *Give me $19.99 a month*.

There were many facilities that raised money or operated in a way I didn't agree with, but you know what? They might not agree with what I did all the time, so I just kept my mouth shut and did my own thing. But Carole, her facility was run the exact same way as mine. What a hypocrite she was to try to shut me down for doing the same things she seems to have done.

I was desperate to find ways to fight back against Carole. One day I found a photo on Facebook of one of Carole's staff on the back of a golf cart, holding up bloody rabbit bodies and laughing about it. It was disgusting. I sent that picture to every rabbit rescue I could find, and they gave Carole hell. But this bitch Carole Baskin, she could teach the devil a few tricks. She bought that picture from the volunteer for $5, copyrighted it three months after I posted it, then sued me for copyright infringement.

Along with that, Carole sued me over a trademark. She had her logo with a tiger jumping over the words "Big Cat Rescue." I came up with a logo called "Big Cat Rescue Entertainment," with snow leopard eyes behind it. No jumping tiger.

Even though the trademark office said Carole held no claim

to the words "Big Cat Rescue" without a tiger leaping over them, Carole filed a lawsuit and easily outspent us in court. She filed both these suits basically at the same time, and not just against me; she also sued a couple of my employees, and Finlay, and even my mother.

Finally I'd had enough. I wanted to start fighting back. Myself, Finlay, and Rink went to Tampa, Florida, to Big Cat Rescue, and paid to go on a tour of her "sanctuary."

What is a sanctuary? To me, it's when a private owner doesn't want to pay for their animal-hoarding problem. So they file for a nonprofit, pay the $850 fee, and then get people to pay for their hobby and lifestyle. That, ladies and gentlemen, is all a sanctuary is.

Finlay and Rink had both seen Carole's park before, but this was my first time. But before we even got to the park, we were contacted by a former employee of Carole's. I'd spoken to her previously, and when I told her we were coming to town, she agreed to meet with me to discuss some information she had on Carole.

I met this woman at a restaurant, where she gave me over a thousand documents, including Carole's personal diary and lots of bank statements and receipts. There were a lot of receipts for the purchase of supposedly "rescued" cats. A whole lot.

Now here we were on this tour of Big Cat Rescue. We went in through a gift shop and out into a tiny yard where they held us until the tour started. That's where all the propaganda began about how bad private breeders are, but the whole time I was looking over their wooden fences, seeing what looked to me like rusty cages with weeds and grass five feet high in and around them.

The tour started and we got to this black leopard cage, which was just wire around a rock. The leopard looked sick, his eyes sunken in his head. The tour guide told us they'd rescued him from the pet trade, but I had what I believe were the papers to prove it was born at Big Cat Rescue, bred from other leopards Carole had.

Then we noticed this old lady using a long pole to scoop poop out of one of the cages. They never went in to clean the whole cage; they just used poop poles. We posted videos on my YouTube channel of the water being pumped from the pond—the junkyard pond—through all the cat cages in a cement trench. Keep in mind all big cats shit and pee in the water, as it hides the smell like in the wild. That filthy water was being shared from cage to cage.

The real topper to me was a white tiger they had, with a photo of Kenny, the white tiger with the birth defect, posted next to his cage. It seemed to me to be such a boldfaced lie, to use Kenny's picture to raise money off this perfectly normal white tiger.

In all we saw about thirteen cats, most of them small. As we were finishing up, I noticed a white wooden cross over in the woods. I hollered to Rink and Finlay, "There's Don's grave!" The whole group started laughing. I introduced myself in front of everyone and yelled, "Everything the guide just said was a lie!"

I walked out of the park as soon as I did it, and when I left I was beside myself because I thought it was such a shithole and full of lies—the whole tour was lies. To me, they were lying to people who didn't know any better; the whole thing was a scam. I had the receipts in the car in their parking lot! I knew where these animals came from: Carole had bought them.

Soon after that we went back, got a permit, and protested outside of Big Cat Rescue. I dressed up in a giant white rabbit suit, with blood all over me, and posed in front of Big Cat Rescue's driveway. Every person who drove by honked and yelled out, "She killed her husband!"

To hear Carole tell the story about us out there protesting, it was a threat on her life. Listen up, crackhead: We were standing on a public sidewalk with a permit to protest and a cop car parked there the whole time. I was in a fucking bunny suit—like, who the hell wouldn't notice me there?

Does anyone really think I was there as a threat to Carole's physical safety? Or to just see how Carole liked someone fucking with *her* business? People in this country always think it's okay for them to mess with someone, but when the shoe is on the other foot, it's all *poor me.*

Carole filed suit after suit, withdrawing them right before trial and suing again a month later. For all the nasty things I say about her, I have to give it to her: Carole is a smart lady. Smart as a fox. It was running me over half a million dollars fighting this shit. We had to hire four law firms to represent us and I took some bad legal advice. I thought I could let her get a judgment out on me, and then I'd file bankruptcy and the judgment would go away.

That's why I agreed to settle, and ended up owing her a million dollars. It didn't work out the way I thought it would. Because Carole never goes away. Money was apparently no object to her. Now do you call that obsessed?

There was one good thing I guess I could say that came out of Carole's suing me. Me and Finlay flew down to Tampa to do depositions, and after they were over we went to eat with some friends. We pulled into a parking lot and a lady was running around screaming with this baby in her arms and I just acted without even thinking and grabbed the child out of her arms—he couldn't have been two years old, if that—and he was choking on food and was unconscious and not breathing. I reached in his mouth and pushed the food on down his throat and did CPR and got him breathing before the ambulance got there. He made it, and he should be about eighteen years old now.

A million-dollar lawsuit in exchange for saving the life of a baby? I can live with that. Especially because Carole never got her million dollars anyway.

It was becoming impossible to book and keep any shows on the road. Anytime someone would take a chance on us, they'd get bombarded by Carole and her goons, and they'd back out. I even booked shows where I'd just have music and magic, with no tigers, no animals, and Carole still couldn't leave me alone or let me be. I had no choice but to shut down the show.

We did our last tour forty-two weeks straight in 2011, and finished with a seventeen-day festival in Las Vegas. I chased my drunken crew around that town every day. It was such a mess. When I got back to Oklahoma I parked the truck, sold as much of the set pieces as I could, and never took the whole magic show out again.

In the end, Carole won because she got what she seemed to want: she got my road show canceled for good. I wasn't giving up, though. I just had to shift my focus. Now that I was off the road I could concentrate on the zoo, and making my shows there bigger and better. The shows on the road were all with small animals like rabbits, monkeys, and doves. The shows at the park didn't have as much magic in them, but we had all our full-grown tigers that loved me.

I was sure we could come up with a great show. I needed to elevate my customer's experience, though, so I asked a good friend of mine, Doc Antle, if he could help me. He invited me to come stay at his beautiful sanctuary in South Carolina and relax for a little bit. Finlay, Paul, Rink, and I all went to Doc's to check it out.

Doc is the only person in the exotic animal industry who will take time out of his own day to teach others how to be better animal advocates, and how to make a captive animal's life more enjoyable. He had been in the business twice as long as I had, and his animals were much more expensive than mine. He also had three girlfriends living with him on his property, and they all seemed to exist in peace and harmony.

Holy shit, what an experience Doc's park was. We got to swim with Bubbles the elephant, and I got to know an orangutan named Hanuman. Bubbles was amazing, so gentle about everything she did. In the river, she'd pick us up with her trunk and throw us over her back. Every time she did that to one of us, she would go completely below water and blow bubbles and roll around like she was laughing her ass off. Elephants not only have souls, they have feelings, like humans; they feel emotional pain and happiness, and they have fun and laugh in their own way, with no sound coming out.

Doc has the connection with animals that few of us do. It drives people like Carole batshit crazy that we get in with our tigers and walk them around our parks and she can't. To me, his place felt safe, like I could really relax with his animals (even the ones I couldn't afford). He gave me a lot of great advice on that trip—about life, and about my zoo. He told me to spend more time with my customers, making their experience more interactive. He also told me to quit killing myself working day and night, having so many animals people would never see. Hell, I had hamsters, guinea pigs, and all kinds of shit that people didn't come to a zoo to see. I loved them but had to get my priorities straight.

After I got back, I sat down with Rink and Mom and came up with a plan for how to take our park to the next level. I did as Doc had suggested, and gave away all the small animals and directed my attention toward the large ones. They were the key to paying the bills at the zoo. I applied every ounce of advice Doc gave me, including some simple ways to make my zoo more beautiful, and my business tripled. We went from tours of thirty or so people to bringing in over one hundred people at a time.

Sure, I'd had my livelihood taken away from me by Carole's lawsuits, but I had found a new one, with hundreds of paying guests coming through each week. I had two loving partners, and a whole zoo to keep me busy. I felt good. It felt like maybe things were going to turn around for Joe Exotic. Little did I know how badly the shit was about to hit the fan.

# CHAPTER 13

Now that I didn't have the road show anymore, I found myself aching for ways to connect with more people. I figured I could do an online show. That way I could still interact with fans, and it's not like Carole could have me banned from YouTube (you never know anymore, though).

There was another reason for the show: I wanted people to know who they were dealing with when they messed with my park.

See, we were always dealing with crazy people, and I'm not just talking about my employees. Carole and PETA had listed me as their most-wanted animal abuser, and all I did was let people pet baby tigers. There were a lot of unhinged and uninformed people who had a problem with my park.

PETA sent people undercover all the time. At least they claimed to be from PETA—who knows? There was always someone trying to break into the park and start trouble. A couple of these crazy people made a video in front of my park. They killed chinchillas, made a gruesome video, and had my park's sign in the background, trying to make it look like these animals died under my watch.

The cops busted them, but they were let go. No consequences, except for the ones I had to face. People didn't know the image was fake. Shit, who the fuck thinks to question every single picture you see, to make sure it's telling you something true? Not even the *New York Times* knows how to do that shit.

One day a man came into the zoo at 8 a.m. and threatened to kill Rink and let all the animals out. By the time an officer arrived, my staff had come to Rink's rescue and tackled the man and put him in cuffs. He broke one of my staff member's arms. The Garvin County Sheriff refused to press charges. I paid for the broken arm.

There were multiple death threats made against me, all of which I contacted the FBI about. One threat I got was that a group of people was going to come into the zoo at night and kill all of us, and the cats. They said they'd be able to get it all done and be out of the park within one hour. The FBI didn't even come talk to us.

Bottom line, I needed to keep my staff and my animals safe. These animal rights activists would welcome the chance to harm my animals, if they could blame it on me and shut me down. They tried doing it all the time. I didn't know how to handle the full-blown stupidity. But it occurred to me that if these crazy people saw me acting like an even crazier bastard on YouTube, maybe they'd be less likely to break in.

I did some crazy shit on YouTube and social media. I video-taped everything that happened at the park and then I'd put it up online without editing it. I'd also do a daily talk show kind of thing, where I'd talk a lot about Carole and how much I hated her guts. I never hurt anyone nor did I plan to hurt anyone. Acting crazy was the only way to keep the haters from coming after my zoo. If you ever watch my old YouTube shows, whichever ones are still up and running, you'll see that I say—often and loudly—that I would shoot anyone who tried to illegally enter my zoo.

It worked for the most part. People stopped sneaking in. I still couldn't control the undercover people. Whenever I had a problem with an employee, they'd threaten to run to Carole and tell her everything. I'd say to go right ahead and tell her whatever they want. Very often they did.

Now that I had a film crew, I started doing my own music and music videos, too. I met this amazing man from Washington state named Danny who helped me write some of my songs and did some of the backup vocals with me. That became an amazing friendship and we made a good team because we would sing together and we sounded identical. My first song was "GW and Me," which I recorded in a studio in Dallas, Texas. Some of my favorites were "My First Love," "The Sun Says," which was for my dad, and my all-time favorite, "This Old Town."

A lot of television shows wanted to come in and showcase our park for their viewers. I found out quickly that these people would often try to make you look stupid and like an animal abuser. So I had a rule that whenever a film company came, I filmed them filming me. Then if they tried to edit something to make me look bad, I'd release the uncut truth online. The footage my film crew was capturing was fantastic, and I realized I could probably have a hit show, something like *Deadliest Catch*, which I thought was great.

*Joe Exotic Speaks* was a show I'd do every day, where I would expose the scams in the animal industry. For example, Carole says it costs $10,000 to feed one tiger for a year. Remember I am in prison and they don't make calculators accessible here, but the USDA only allows you to feed a full-grown tiger twelve pounds a day, six days a week, so that is what, seventy-two pounds a week per tiger. We buy chicken for thirty-eight cents a pound. That's close to $2,000 per year. And that's not counting freebies like road-kill, dead horses, and donated cows. So, in theory, when Carole raises $10,000 to feed a tiger, $2,000 of it goes toward feeding the tiger, and she's left with $8,000 per tiger.

I was getting so much alleged dirt on Carole Baskin from some of the many people whose lives she destroyed.

I had names and dates from Carole's allegedly predatory lend-ing, where she would sell a house to a couple that could not get credit, and she would draw up such a long note that they didn't read the whole thing through, and after the down payment and a year or two of payments, she'd increase the monthly amounts so much that she knew no one could keep up, so she got to keep the down payment and repo the house and sell it again. I think she is a master at screwing people over, and I bet when people read this book, they will come out of the woodwork again with stories, dates, and amounts.

I made a YouTube video at the Hillsborough County Sheriff's Office when we filed over sixty counts of alleged notary fraud against Carole. Nothing ever came of it.

In my opinion, after Don Lewis went missing and Carole in-herited six million or so from his estate, she didn't need to do all the things the rest of us had to do to support our animals. And then she found it easier to bash others for what she used to do and get free donations from across the world. It was easy. Very few people would really ever show up to see the truth of what Big Cat Rescue was.

I'm telling you: Carole was no different than any other private animal owner, except for the level of vindictiveness seared deep into her bones. It's my opinion that she had a personal vendetta against me and was fixated on destroying me, not because of the way I treated my animals, but because I was exposing her true apparent intentions to the world. Carole knows that the more people knew the truth about how close I was with my animals, the more it would ruin her fundraising off of throwing dirt on my name. And she especially hated the hybrids, probably because she couldn't breed them without violating her own rules. If she couldn't have them, she didn't want anyone else to have them, either.

People often ask me, *Why tigers and lions*? *How could this be worth so much money?* Pay attention to what I'm saying to you here: people love big cats and will travel thousands of miles to see them. The more laws people like Carole can lobby to change, the more they can create a monopoly for their own organizations.

Which brings us to the event that really changed everything—one of the worst days in the history of the exotic animal industry. October 18, 2011: the Zanesville Animal Massacre at Thompson Farm.

I'd met the ill-fated Terry Thompson a couple times, at the exotic animal auction in Mt. Hope, Ohio. I knew him by name much better; his private collection of animals was well regarded.

I got a call one night from a friend of mine, who was up at Terry's zoo. Terry was in prison for a federal weapons charge, and his animals were being watched by a bunch of drunken teenagers.

My friend was with the game warden, and they were calling to ask if I'd come take the animals.

Of course I said yes. We were getting ready to head up to Ohio when I got another call, this one from the local sheriff up there, name of Sheriff Lutz. Lutz told us to pack it up and turn back around because we had no right to move the animals. He was wrong—a game warden outranks a cop or a sheriff—but he clearly felt strong in his conviction that he didn't want us up at Thompson Farm, so we did not go.

Shortly after, Terry got out of prison. Less than a month later, he was dead, along with almost every single one of his animals.

According to the police, Terry had opened most of his animal cages, and then shot and killed himself. It was assumed that Terry had planned to wreak havoc on the town of Zanesville by letting his animals loose. But something about all this didn't seem right to me.

I drove up to Zanesville with a film crew, to see what I could suss out. We walked up a neighbor's land and I lay on my belly to get closer to the cages Terry had. Terry's farm was on a bunch of acres of green pasture with soft, rolling hills, and the house, barn, and cages were set pretty far back off the highway. The cages were small, nothing fancy, and there were a lot of junk cars scattered throughout the property.

There are so many questions that were never brought to light about the tragedy that happened in Zanesville. The first thing anyone who has exotic animals knows is that if you let them out, they are going to be slaughtered. If you care about your animals, you would never do that, and according to people who knew Terry, he loved his animals. So that didn't make sense.

Also, it appeared Terry had shot himself with his left hand, even though he was right-handed, and his left hand was injured. Then come to find out, most of the cages hadn't been unlocked; they'd been cut apart. Surely Terry had the keys, so why would he go through the extra time and energy it would take to cut the cages open?

Out of fifty-six lions, tigers, and bears, only six survived. The surviving animals seemed like they were in good shape. There were two spotted leopards, a black leopard, a grizzly bear, and two apes. Strangely, these were the most expensive animals on the property. Unlike full-grown lions and tigers, adult leopards are actually worth something when they're full-grown. And the apes were worth about $10,000 apiece.

Some people think Terry opened those cages to commit death by suicide. If that were the case, or if Terry's motive really was to wreak havoc on his community, he would've let the most aggressive animals loose. The leopards would be the deadliest and the hardest to track, and they hadn't even been let out of their cages.

The local police made no attempt to keep any of these animals alive. They could have called the Columbus Zoo, run by Jack Hanna, and had all the animals tranquilized, but instead they shot everything dead. In many of the cages that were opened that day, the animals never even came out. They were too scared to leave their cage, but the police still saw them as a big enough threat to shoot them, in their cages. Even baby cubs were shot in their cages. I know this for a fact; I saw the pictures myself.

And then, the most damning evidence against the theory that Terry had gone nuts and done all this himself—Terry's body was found with his pants and underwear around his ankles. A white tiger was eating his genitals when his body was found.

Now tell me, who would expose their genitals like that right before shooting themselves? It made no sense. I had more tigers than anyone in the world, and there is no way a tiger is going to unzip your pants and pull them down past your knees before they start to eat you. A tiger would begin with your head and neck and hands first; it wouldn't have taken his pants down.

Terry's good friend John Moore, who'd helped take care of the animals, tried to reenact Terry's actions, and opened up all the cages in the timeframe that Terry supposedly had done it. See, we know Terry was alive at three in the afternoon, and his body was found at five thirty that same day. That only gave him two hours and thirty minutes to pull off everything they accused him of. The timing didn't work out.

I even found out that some tiger cubs were removed from the property the day before the massacre, and hidden in the kitchen of a neighbor's home. This was all planned very carefully; they just didn't factor in the wild card, Joe Exotic TV, spoiling it all by jumping in the middle, just like I did with Don Lewis's case.

It seemed clear to me there was some kind of conspiracy going on. Terry had been in prison for gun charges, and the gun he shot himself with was apparently registered to a local cop. Maybe he'd gotten mixed up with a dirty cop who was smuggling illegal guns, and the massacre was just a ruse.

If this could happen to Terry Thompson, it could happen to me. I started speaking about his case on my YouTube show. I started speaking to the press, to anyone who would listen, and sharing my theory that the Zanesville Massacre was a setup and that Terry Thompson did not kill himself. Everyone thought I was crazy, except Terry's wife, Marian, and Terry's friend, John Moore. Marian messaged me on Facebook and asked me not to give up fighting for Terry. John Moore came on my YouTube show, "Joe Speaks Out," and shared more of the details about what had happened. I even wrote and recorded a music video for a song, "You Can't Believe:"

> *They can come for you and come for me*
> *Dripped in self-righteous democracy*
> *In this wasteland of the free, America my country*
> *You can't believe all you see*
> *You can't believe all you read*
> *I knew the man, I know the drill*
> *There's something wrong in Zanesville*

Prophetic, isn't it? There's something wrong in this whole damn country.

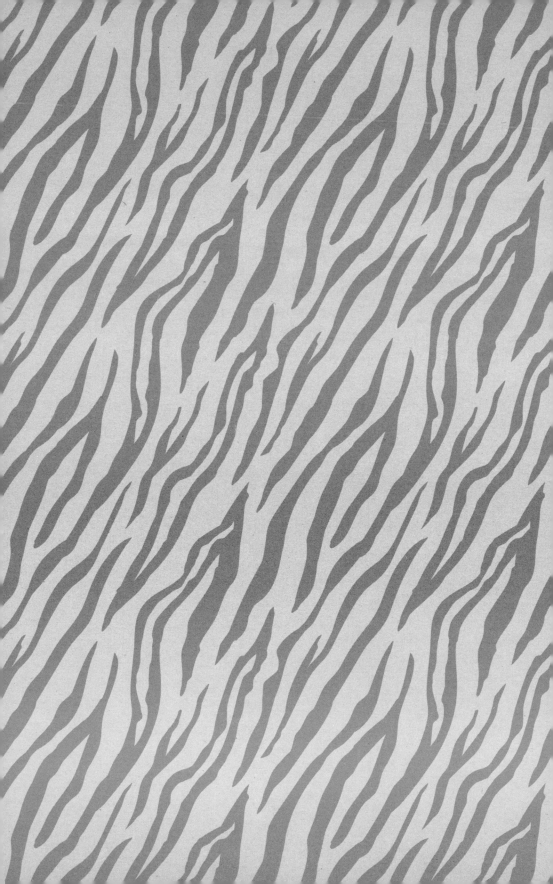

# CHAPTER 14

All the newspapers thought I was crazy for linking Zanesville to the animal rights movement. And yet, a month and a half after the Zanesville Massacre, then–Ohio State Senator Troy Balderson, a Zanesville resident, proposed a statewide ban on exotic animals. There was to be a hearing on Senate Bill 310, the Dangerous Wild Animal Act.

It was all over the news that PETA and the GFAS—Global Federation of Animal Sanctuaries—were pushing for this emergency ban law. I heard Carole was going to be there, speaking on behalf of the ban. Well, of course she'd want to ban tigers in Ohio; her sanctuary is in Florida. She was trying to ban her competition. You will never see Carole or her buddies fight to introduce laws in their own states to ban exotic animals, or make the regulations harder.

If Carole was going to be testifying for the ban, I sure as shit was going to be testifying, too. I went up there in March 2012, wearing my park uniform, which was a light tan shirt and tan Wranglers. Carole wore her uniform, a brown leopard-print blouse and black slacks. I bet her closet looks like Hobby Lobby with all the flowers and animal prints.

The Senate hearing was in a small committee room, maybe one hundred people in there fighting both sides. Senator Balderson and a few other senators were seated like a city council up front. It went on for a couple days.

When it was my turn to talk, I told the committee what was really going on here: This was all about certain people getting rich. This ban had nothing to do with helping animals. It was about so-called nonprofit organizations like the GFAS and the AZA (Association of Zoos and Aquariums) creating a monopoly.

The proposed bill would ban private ownership of exotics in Ohio, but it would override USDA guidelines and exempt GFAS and AZA facilities. This seemed to me like a clear case of private entities taking out their competition with the help of government agencies.

I also spoke at the hearing on behalf of Terry Thompson, whose so-called insanity had been used to rush through this ban law. It was—and remains—my belief that he was murdered, and that people involved in drafting this animal ban could also have been involved with that murder.

They didn't care. I could see it in their eyes. Nothing I could say would change their minds; the right palms had probably already been greased.

Carole testified on behalf of the GFAS, and she went on and on about her damn Big Cat Public Safety Act, a federal version of the Ohio bill. She talked about how dangerous we all are with tigers, and how private owners shouldn't have them. She made it out like she was the expert on tigers and the rest of us were just stupid.

When the final day of the hearing ended, Carole, her associate from the GFAS, and I were standing in the back of the room with a few other people. I was explaining the harmful nature of the proposed ban to someone, and Carole butted in and said, "Oh stop, Joe, you're the one abusing cubs and no one should be petting tigers."

I left it at that. I wasn't going to let her rope me into making a scene in a government building. As soon as she left, I went right back to explaining how she was going to rake in money once this law passed. And I was right. Carole's people may have even helped write the bill, and it conveniently would exempt her and her friends' facilities, like the Columbus Zoo, run by Jack Hanna. Columbus Zoo is where Terry Thompson's surviving expensive animals were sent. I hate Jack Hanna, because I hate hypocrites. He rents animals from different zoos to go on the late shows with, then accuses the rest of us of exploiting animals. That bastard may even be in bed with Carole.

A couple months after the hearing, the HSUS alleged animal abuse at my park. Strange timing, huh? They'd had an undercover employee working there at the same time Terry Thompson was murdered, and they made this deceptively edited video of me showing the staff how to get a tiger to walk on a leash, with a light tap on the butt. They filed formal complaints with the USDA, the United States Fish and Wildlife Service (FWS), and the Oklahoma Department of Wildlife Conservation, but nothing came of it—not one USDA inspection accused me of any abuse, ever.

The main complaint was that my zoo wasn't safe. I get that they saw it that way, because these people work in corporate buildings, and never really interact with tigers the way I do. They see me in a cage with a tiger and think I'm putting myself and others in danger.

But they didn't know the first thing about me and the relationship I had with my animals.

I had been licensed by the USDA for every type of animal in my possession since I'd run the pet store. Never had I been cited for anything until Carole Baskin started messing with me. For every complaint filed against me, I had to spend an entire day going through an inspection with someone from the USDA, who generally knew much less about the proper care of exotics than I did. Filing complaints felt to me like a game for Carole, the HSUS, PETA, and anyone else who didn't like me.

Less than a month after the HSUS filed their complaints against me, then–Ohio Governor John Kasich signed Senate Bill 310, banning exotic animals in the state. As soon as it was signed, the Ohio Department of Agriculture sent SWAT teams into people's homes. They confiscated exotic animals, and then turned around and gave contracts exclusively to GFAS facilities to haul these lions, tigers, and bears out of Ohio to GFAS facilities in states without exotic animal bans.

For each truckload of stolen animals, these GFAS facilities— namely a place called Lions Tigers & Bears that Carole was probably in cahoots with—were also given $250,000. I've seen the contracts; I filed a Freedom of Information Act request to get them. It was worth millions to these people to have the state of Ohio ban exotic animals.

The newly rescued animals would be broadcast across social media, with sad music playing while a voice-over whines about how nothing can help these tigers except your monetary donations: "Call now." It was, in my mind, all one big racket to steal from honest, hard-working Americans.

I did what I could to help people. I volunteered my services to go out to Ohio to help relocate some animals. That way if the owners were able to beat the ban, or if they moved to another state, they could get their animals back from me, rather than fighting an organization like the GFAS. The Ohio Department of Natural Resources denied me the right to move animals out of Ohio. You can't convince me that some government employees weren't getting a split of all this money. Who the hell gets paid $250K to move a tiger I could move for gas money?

On my online show, we held auctions to raise money for lawyers to fight back. One night we raised $10,000 in two hours, and a lady in Ohio matched it, so we raised $20,000. There was a case already in the courts, with a private owner named Kenny Hetrick who had a place in Ohio called Tiger Ridge Exotics. The government raided him, took all his animals, and was spending a fortune to keep them in facilities out of state. Kenny just wanted his animals back. We sent all the money we raised to his attorneys. If that case had won, it would have overturned the law. It ended up going on for many years, and Kenny never got his animals back.

The AZA and GFAS are the ones creating the guidelines and accreditations, with more power than the government and the USDA. How can a private organization have more power than a government agency? If the government were handling this, we'd all be paying fines instead of turning everything over to PETA and GFAS sanctuaries.

I believe the AZA and GFAS are probably in bed together. From what I know, they made this deal that if they share mutual support, they will leave each other alone. The GFAS takes all the big cats and bears they can raise donations with and the AZA gets all the expensive animals.

Blows my mind how stupid our lawmakers are to go along with this; they will take a tiger that has never hurt anyone, from a private home, and give people like Carole a quarter million dollars to take that tiger and put it on exhibit to sell tickets for tours. This, to me, is stealing, plain and simple.

The HSUS was on my ass from then on, but their problem was they never had any proof of animal abuse against me, because there never was any. I have never been charged with animal cruelty. My tigers loved me. If I abused my tigers, I would not be able to get in the same cage with them and live to tell about it. HSUS couldn't shut me down with complaints, bad press, Carole's lawsuits, or anything else, so they had to set me up.

Ask yourself a question: Why is Carole always left alone by the HSUS and PETA? Because they are all the same. Carole probably gives the HSUS tens of thousands of dollars each year, as a sponsor, and for renting tables at conventions. That might make it legal on paper, but it's still, to me, hush money. That is how she keeps tigers in such shitty cages and they never bitch to her about anything, but the rest of us are evil bastards for caging animals.

Are you starting to understand why they hated me so much? Are you starting to understand why I am here in prison and why the feds made sure I am here? I knew too much and I was on the way to exposing them all. One day, maybe when this book comes out, the world will know the truth. I believe that not only Don Lewis died for this agenda, but so did Terry Thompson. The whole thing makes me sick.

# CHAPTER 15

There was a small zoo in Missouri named D&D Farm and Animal Sanctuary, run by the two nicest people ever, and they were in trouble. Deb and Dale were elderly, and the USDA was citing them; they'd been given three days to get into compliance with USDA laws, or their animals would be taken away.

I did a real quick online show one night, calling for volunteers to meet at D&D to help Deb and Dale get everything up to code. The next day I put two crews from our zoo together and we headed over.

People drove in from many other states to help. Within two days, through pouring rain, all these complete strangers who watched my show had helped me rebuild this entire zoo.

D&D got a completely perfect inspection three days after we met, and they got to not only stay open but keep all their beloved animals.

While I was there, I showed Deb and Dale some easy and more economical ways to take care of their farm and animals. The difference between people like Carole and me is that she loves taking animals away from people, which is hard on not just the owners but also the animals, because animals do go through a grieving process. I specialized in helping people learn what to do to keep their animals.

It is amazing what we were able to build at GW Zoo out of love, and how it brought my parents and me together and helped us survive such tragedy. Helping people get their own zoos in order felt like paying it all forward. We did stuff like this time and time again.

Same thing with the famous Tiger Truck Stop on I-10 in Louisiana—home of Tony the Tiger. PETA and Carole's crowd were all over owner Michael Sandlin for having a tiger on display at the truck stop, and maybe you agree that a tiger shouldn't be at a truck stop. But, folks, let's be clear: Tony the Tiger's compound was nicer than anything Carole's tigers ever lived in. He had air-conditioning, he had heat, and then he had this big grassy area, bigger than a football field. But still, Michael Sandlin was being sued by the Animal Legal Defense Fund, and one of the big complaints against him was that Tony didn't have a pool to cool off in.

This was some ridiculous shit Michael Sandlin had to put up with. I put my construction crew together and we all flew into New Orleans, went to the Tiger Truck Stop, and built Tony a class-act swimming pool in his compound, with a nice big deck so he could lie in the sun.

God does have a funny sense of humor, because Tony (he's passed away now) never went in that pool. Michael says he would lie on the deck and sun himself and just dip the tip of his top claw in and that was it.

But none of this was ever about Tony; seems to me it was about humiliating private owners through frivolous allegations.

Taking care of my own community in Wynnewood was also always on my mind. I cooked for nearly two hundred people every Thanksgiving and Christmas at the zoo. I did a free Easter egg hunt with ten thousand eggs, every year. People say I was all about money and lost focus about what the zoo was built for. Let me tell you, if people knew half of what we did, they would understand why I was always broke.

Then there was always John Finlay and Paul Rowe to take care of. Since we had stopped doing road shows, neither of them seemed to have enough desire to do much of anything at all. That's the problem with being in a relationship with younger people: they have no work ethic.

It also didn't help that they had both been straight before meeting me. Finlay and Paul both claimed to have never been with a man before. I know it wasn't just about me, because they'd have sex with each other sometimes, too. They never told me when they did, but when the door was locked, I knew what it meant. It was far from a perfect home life, but things were okay between us all. I had "John" and "Paul" tattooed on my right arm. Paul tattooed "John" on his left arm and "Joe" on his right arm.

Most of the time with Paul, it was about how much money I could spend on him. Finally, Paul realized there wasn't enough money for him to stick around. He left to go back with his family, where I heard he may have gotten into trouble, got married and divorced within six months, and then went to work for a sanctuary out in Tennessee or Kentucky. I never heard from him again.

Finlay, on the other hand, he never asked for anything. He just wanted to be left alone, and he wanted to do his drugs. Around Davis and Wynnewood, Oklahoma, everyone is into meth and weed. Here we go again. Meth had been a dark, twisted part of my past, but it was the distant past. At least it was, until Finlay brought it back into our lives.

I'm not talking about a daily or even weekly habit for me personally. Maybe once a month, or every other month, we would go get a motel and I would let myself partake. Drugs never were an addiction for me; my addiction was my work. My business always came first, so unless I had a day to leave the zoo, I wasn't about to get high. Besides, the tigers could smell that shit through your pores and they hated it.

Feeling weird is not my thing, but meth is a highly addictive substance, and for some people, once you ring that bell it can't be un-rung. It seemed to me that Finlay could never have enough. He was worse than Brian ever was, and he was doing it with anyone he could.

I started hearing rumors about Finlay having sex with all kinds of different men and women. It was always something. If Finlay wasn't having naked pictures coming in through his PlayStation, they were in his private messages on Facebook. There was a dog-catcher in Davenport, Iowa, that we'd met when we did shows there, and she would send him pictures of her junk that I swear looked like some alien with teeth, it was so big and ugly. Picture Bigfoot bent over with hemorrhoids.

It got so bad that one day I took a sledgehammer to the satellite dish out in the yard. We never had internet at home again. I bet the pieces are still out there.

Then there was this chick named Trixie that Finlay got to come to the house so he could pay her for sex. This is the one time I almost had to go to prison for murder because I did pull my .357 out and run that bitch out of my house.

All this I was willing to put up with. My sense of self-worth was so fucked that I let him treat me as horribly as I was used to. But then he started to shoot steroids, and his personality got darker. He was meaner. Things started to get physical—slowly at first, but then things got worse. Just like I'd always done, I took the beatings and never hit back. Afterward I'd make my way to the emergency room to get stitched up and tell the ER doctor some lie about what happened to me. I didn't want Finlay to get in trouble. I felt bad for him; he was helpless and lashing out. Besides, it was the steroids and the meth and the not-sleeping that was making him crazy—it's not that he was a bad guy. It seemed far better to me, at the time, to put up with the abuse, rather than have to face the thought of being alone.

We had two tigers that grew up in the house with us, Thunder and Lightning: two of my favorite tigers ever. Thunder was orange, and born cross-eyed. Finlay kicked him one day and broke his right hip. We had to have it pinned together.

Finlay was ashamed of himself—he knew he'd fucked up. Later I found him sitting in the primate house with his face in the corner like he'd put himself in time-out. Some creepy, Blair Witch kinda shit right there.

He had that mindset that you can overpower animals. Like people think with horses, you beat them until they become submissive. Sometimes he would flick the nose of a cub if it got too rough. I hated that, and I was always telling him to quit being so rough with the animals. Not just because it's mean but because it's dangerous. If an animal's defensive, it's dangerous.

Boy, did it suck, but I wasn't giving up on Finlay. We weren't married but I wore his ring; we'd made a commitment and I planned to see it through.

Then everything changed in the blink of an eye when a man named Travis Michael Maldonado came into my life.

Travis came to work as a camera guy for my show, and that lasted about one week. He was hard to miss, six foot five and built like a brick shithouse. A wild child from California, he was nineteen, basically homeless, and addicted to meth.

Here I go again, having to save everyone. Despite every red flag available, I fell in love with Travis at first sight. But I would never have dreamed in a million years he would ever think of falling in love with me.

The first day Travis was with us, we were filming hauling trash to the back of the zoo. He was on the trailer, holding the camera, and I asked him, "How straight are you?"

He said, "Pretty straight."

I said, "Do you watch porn?" and he nodded yes, and I said, "Do you like watching the ones with the big dicks or the little ones?"

He said, "The big ones."

"The big ones give you an erection? Then you're not that straight, are ya?"

That made him laugh, and I could see in his eyes that he liked me. We talked for a long time that night and told each other everything. I told him about GW, and JC, and Paul Rowe and Finlay. He told me about his family, his meth-head mother who fed him drugs like vitamins, and the abuse he suffered at the hands of his family's friends.

I told him that if he wanted to get off meth I'd help him do it. He asked me if I'd ever be open to being in a three-way relationship again. I said I'd have to ask Finlay about it, and he said that sounded like a good idea. Finlay agreed to have Travis come live with us and see where it went. He didn't care—all he did was play PlayStation and sleep. A week later Travis moved in.

I could tell right away that something was wrong with Travis. The next morning, he was sitting on the tailgate of the pickup under the carport, and I went out to talk to him and see what he was struggling with.

He was very calm, which wasn't like him; usually he was going ninety miles a minute. But he told me he was worried—he didn't want to let his guard down because we had known each other only a couple weeks and slept with each other only one night.

"Can you really fall in love with another man that quick?" he said. This poor guy didn't know if he could believe my love was real or not! Clearly he didn't know me yet, because as he'd soon come to recognize, my *real* superpower is how much love I have in my heart, especially for the helpless. Connecting with the animals is just a byproduct of that.

"You are going to be so easy to fall in love with," I said to him, and it was the truth.

It wasn't even a few weeks after Travis and I got into a relationship that he saved my life. I was doing a show at the zoo and at that time I used a tiger named Sarge, who had never given me a problem before, ever. I was about to get off the stage with Sarge right beside me, when he suddenly locked eyes on me and got down on his front legs in pounce mode. Something bad was about to happen. My whole body winced, waiting to die, when out of nowhere Travis grabbed a fire extinguisher and shot it in Sarge's face, sending Sarge running back to his cage.

Travis wasn't even working at the zoo officially yet, and he had never been trained to do something like that. Damn, he was watching my back better than people who were paid to do so! That was the one and only time he had to save my life and boy, was he put there for a reason.

If you ever watched *The Beverly Hillbillies*, that was Travis, just like Jethro. He was my mountain man—he loved his four-wheeler, his dune buggy, and his guns. He'd eat anything and refused to use silverware; he only ate with his giant hands, and drank from the milk carton, never a glass. Wouldn't wear new pants for anything; his favorite pants had the zipper held together with a shoestring. I thought he was perfect just the way he was. For the first time ever, I woke up every morning excited for life, because I knew what falling in true love was all about.

Do you wonder why someone would need a third person in a relationship? Well, it's usually because something is missing, or the love is not deep enough for just two people. There was always something missing with Finlay and me—we both knew it—but we supported each other as best we could, at least for a while.

The love I had for Travis was unlike anything I'd felt for Finlay or Paul, or even for Brian. But I'd made a commitment to Finlay, and that's why, when I asked Travis to marry me, I also asked Finlay. They both said yes.

People came from all over the United States for that wedding, including our friends and neighbors in Wynnewood, which was a true miracle, considering we were in the Bible Belt. Lots of our friends brought their animals, including several monkeys, and we even had a Celebes macaque walk down the aisle to hand us our wedding rings. All three of us were dressed in black pants with pink shirts, which was the same thing Brian and I had worn at our wedding. Finlay's mom gave him away, Travis's sister flew in to give him away, my mom gave me away, and my dad even came, which was freaking amazing.

There was just one challenge that had to be overcome before we could know true wedded bliss: the meth addiction.

The only way I knew to get Travis cleaned up was to control his usage of it for him. That meant that at first he was allowed to use, but only in a controlled environment. Basically he was allowed to use two days a week, but only in the house, and only a certain amount. That way he could quell the urge and lose only one night of sleep. We started weaning him off little by little, week by week.

In order for this to work, I had to know where Travis was just about every minute of the day. You can't trust a meth addict. It's not personal; it's just the drug is too strong and they'll lie to anyone if they think they can figure out a way to get a fix.

People gave me such a hard time about controlling Travis and having to know everywhere he went and with who, like I was scared he was going to cheat on me—but it was really so I knew if he was doing meth. After a while I got to know the signs of when he was and wasn't high, so it was hard for him to use without me knowing.

Travis had a terrible time sleeping, and as he got sober, it turned out he was suffering from some PTSD, due to some things he'd gone through as a kid. It got worse when his mother moved into the park and started working for me. I ended up having to fire her after I caught her smoking meth in the commissary one day while she was fixing the animal diets. I knew as long as she was at the zoo I wouldn't be able to get him clean.

After a few months we were able to cut his usage down to one day a week, then twice a month, then one day a month, to the point he could do without it. I wouldn't say he became a whole new person, but it was like the real Travis had been let go from some demonic possession. He had new interests, he got more involved with his dune buggy at the river, and he spent a lot of time making a four-wheeler course and shooting range at the lake.

It was a tough battle, and he fought it one step at a time. I was so proud of him. I think he knew he could trust me, and with that trust he found love for me that was deep in his heart. He was, at the very least, in love with me enough that he was motivated to clean up and make a new life for himself.

If I told you how he came out of his shell . . . when we met he was like a robot. Now he was responsive and loving with everything he did. It was like a male version of *I Dream of Jeannie*—except he was free, of course. To celebrate his new successes, Travis and I went up to Doc Antle's place. Finlay was out on the road but he met us there, too.

It was a tough trip because Travis was enjoying himself so much, going on a tour and swimming with Bubbles the elephant, while Finlay was going off the deep end. The steroids he was taking were going to his head and he was screaming and yelling at people the whole time. Doc even saw Finlay hit me, which was embarrassing because I had a lot of respect for Doc and wanted him to respect me, too. He didn't say anything about it, but when it was time to go, Doc pulled me aside and told me to cut Finlay loose and just stick with Travis. "You're always killing yourself for other people; do what makes you happy for once," he said.

After we got back to our zoo, Finlay's abuse got even worse. He was a madman—I would wake up in the middle of the night and he would be standing at the foot of the bed just staring, waiting to fight, like fucking JC all over again.

Travis knew it was complicated and tried to stay out of it. He asked me a couple times if I wanted him to take care of it, but I always said no, because Finlay was sick, very sick in the head.

Then Finlay finally beat me so bad that I thought he broke my back. I told the ER doctor that I'd fallen off the roof, but I think he knew I was lying.

All of us knew that was the last straw. Finlay admitted he needed professional help and was willing to go to rehab. I took him to three different hospitals to get him admitted for mental help, but no one would take him because he wasn't suicidal. We wised up enough, and Finlay drove himself to the Pauls Valley ER and told them he was going to kill himself. They called the cops and took him to a place called Red Rock in Norman, Oklahoma, for thirty days.

Travis was never abusive, ever. Not one time did we ever even have an argument. Neither of us thought it was worth the energy.

My favorite memory of Travis, I'll never forget, we were driving around town one weekend, heading home on a dusky summer night. Selena came on the radio: "Dreaming of You," one of my favorite songs.

"What do you want to do?" I said, genuinely interested in what he was thinking and feeling at that moment.

He looked at me and said, "Can I just be myself?"

And I said, "Of course, that's all I want from you."

He rolled the window down and stuck his head out like a dog and screamed at the top of his lungs. From that day on he yelled just to hear himself yell everywhere he went.

# CHAPTER 16

Finlay came back after thirty days, clean but still in need of professional help. We'd only been married three months so far and things had fallen apart spectacularly. He was supposed to be helping run the zoo but never got out of bed before four in the afternoon.

Things finally came to a head one day when one of the young employees at the park approached me with fear in his eyes. He had something to tell me and I could tell it wasn't good.

"I just saw John Finlay kissing Amber in the office," he said.

"You've gotta be shitting me."

Amber was supposed to be my secretary, running the front desk! She'd decorated everything for the wedding; who would have known she was going to decorate Finlay with her fat naked body? I ran into the office and the two of them were both acting like they were busy doing some other shit. I called them out on it, told them I knew what was going on, and left the room, trying to hold on to my dignity.

Finlay came running out, passed right by me, and found the employee who snitched on him and beat the hell out of him. I wasn't sure what to do, but I was fed up. I decided it was time to let Finlay go, from my bedroom and my zoo. He didn't take the news so well. The police had to get involved and Finlay was arrested for assault.

I neglected to mention, Amber was married, too. But that didn't stop her from moving Finlay in with her and her husband over in Elmore City. I tried to warn him that Amber and Finlay were fucking, but the cuckold didn't want to believe it. He said Finlay and Amber were just friends and I was just jealous because Finlay had left me.

All Finlay cared about was what felt good to stick his dick in, and let me tell you, he had no taste at all because I could probably come up with over seventy people Finlay had sex with that I know of.

Even though he was gone, I was still kept abreast of what was going on with him and Amber because his phone was connected to the office computer through iCloud. Every time he took a picture it came up on my computer. That's how I found out Amber was pregnant, when they uploaded a video holding a ring over Amber's belly to see if the baby would be a boy or girl.

Can you believe Amber spent nine months sleeping side by side with her husband, and he had no idea she was even pregnant? She was that overweight. She and Finlay went to Ardmore and had the baby, then brought it home and convinced her husband it was Finlay's niece they had to take care of. Guess who had to man up and apologize to me in the Walmart parking lot once he found out who the dad was on the birth certificate? Finlay and Amber finally had to get a place of their own. Stupid rednecks.

As all this was going down, I got very, very sick. Extremely ill. I threw up for six months straight. I went to the doctor and my T-cells and white blood cell counts were off the chart. Automatically it was assumed I had AIDS, but I told them I didn't think that was likely. I took nine HIV tests within probably four months, and every one of them came back negative.

The next idea was cancer. They did several tests, and then I had prostate surgery on October 21, 2014. It didn't go well. I got septic and all my organs quit. I went into kidney and liver failure and spent almost thirty-seven days in the ICU and in the hospital there.

Travis was at the hospital with me, and Finlay and Amber both came by, too. We were all fighting, yelling at each other in the hospital, and I realized: I was on dialysis, and I could barely breathe, I was in so much pain. Why the fuck was I wasting my dying breaths fighting with these people?

The hospital called in a disease specialist to run some tests, and—because the world is truly a small place—it was a woman named Mary who I knew very well because she used to treat Brian. When she came into the ICU she was floored to see me, and at death's door, no less.

"Must be something real bad that could take you down," she said.

Every test imaginable was run on me. I was properly diagnosed with Common Variable Immune Deficiency and hemoglobin anemia. All that means is my bone marrow does not produce blood correctly. Every four weeks for the rest of my life I'd need to get blood transfusions.

God and I had a lot of talks while I was in the hospital. I came to the conclusion life is too short to hold grudges. Travis helped me a lot with this, too. He'd gone through so much, and a big part of his recovery was about letting go of the things he couldn't control. He was a great influence on me and really calmed me down.

One of the first things I did when I was out of the hospital was write and record a song called "Guardians of Children," about a local biker group that advocated for abused and displaced children. Finlay and Amber's baby had been born only a week before, but I called and asked if she could be in the video. That was the first time I got to meet baby Kimber. It was love at first sight.

Neither Finlay nor Amber ever apologized to me. Amber eventually came back to work at the zoo in the office and that is basically where Kimber was raised. She took her first steps to me. Six months down the road Finlay and Amber were fighting like cats and dogs because playtime was over and now life was boring, paying bills and being stuck with each other.

When they split up, Amber tried talking shit about Finlay, and I rubbed it in her face every time: "You thought he hung the moon when you were taking him away from me, but now that you are ready for a new one, all you do is talk shit about him." That is how she is, never happy with anyone.

Kimber for the next three years became a big part of my life no matter who I was with. Travis accepted her as our niece and loved her as much as I did. She knew the words to every song I wrote when she was only two years old. Smart as a whip and got the good looks of Uncle Joe. Every time her music video came on in the gift shop, Kimber would get so excited to see herself on television.

Me and that kid were so close. I loved her like she was my own. I felt sorry for her because neither of her parents seemed to understand what a stable home would ever be, but I was determined to show her true love no matter what.

In all, our three-way marriage only lasted all of eight months, but I will cherish getting married to both Finlay and Travis, as they taught me so much about myself. Finlay left and gave me that beautiful little girl to help raise. And then Travis was enough—he was the first person who made me feel like I was enough, like I was worthy of real, happy love. All the time I'd been married to Brian, and all the years I'd spent with Finlay, there was always something missing. Travis and I lived our lives so, so in love. I didn't need anyone else. Our text messages only said, "I love you hun," back and forth. To hear the words "I love you": that is my drug of choice.

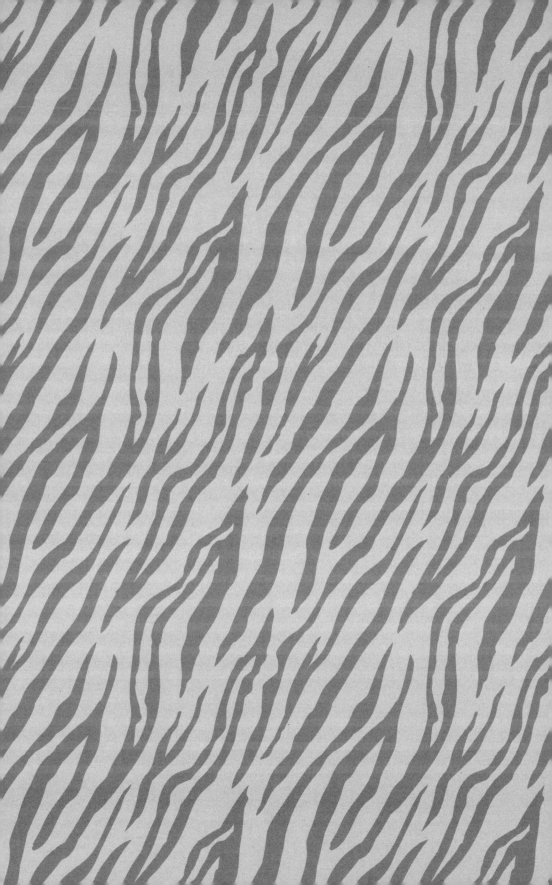

# CHAPTER 17

The USDA was hosting the Lions, Tigers and Bears Symposium, and all their main speakers were from the GFAS. Why would a private organization like the GFAS have anything at all to do with teaching a government entity like the USDA how to properly care for animals? Shouldn't it have been the other way around?

I intended to attend the symposium and continue my work exposing all these apparent scams. So what did they do? Someone called the USDA and told them I threatened to bomb the event. With no proof or nothing, they banned me from coming, and implemented draconian security protocols to search people who wanted to attend. This stopped all the private owners from coming, since I wouldn't be there and since many of them always carried concealed weapons and now wouldn't be able to get into the event with their firearms.

The whole symposium ended up being Carole Baskin and her friends bad-mouthing private owners. Someone secretly videoed the whole thing and made it public, including a speech given by a

GFAS member who admitted they all got in this business because they like money.

After that, every time the USDA inspected my park, they brought an armed wildlife officer with them. Not because of any actual threats I had made, but because of all these lies. They said they needed an armed officer because I was exercising my right in Oklahoma to carry a firearm on my property, and they tried to make it out like I was purposefully intimidating people. That's not what I kept myself armed for; I was in charge of a zoo with over two hundred tigers. If one of my employees screwed up and let some tigers out of their cages, I needed to be able to gain control of my park.

The problem for me was, no matter what anyone did at my zoo, it was me who would be blamed for it. If someone got hurt, it was my fault. I tried to get my employees to follow the rules, but it was next to impossible. They hated me for just asking them to take pride in what they did for a living. The zoo employees were oftentimes more out of control than the animals.

Keep in mind most all these people were drug addicts, alcoholics, and either out of prison or out of rehab and couldn't stay out of trouble. I had Dacus Bail Bonds on speed dial. Some of these people I'd gifted with not only a job but a home, and a new family of animals that never judged them, even when their own families had thrown them out and left them with nowhere to go.

I had to be a father, a mother, a friend, a boss, a psychotherapist, and a counselor, and keep them off drugs and drinking all at one time. It was tiring—no one ever cut me a break—and when things got out of control and I had to fire someone, I was always the bad guy. They stuck together like a pack of wolves; never did the pack back me up.

One zoo employee who gave me nothing but trouble was Erik Cowie; you met him on *Tiger King*. He may look like Jesus Christ with his long, dirty hair, but unlike Jesus, Erik's never done nothing for humanity. Everyone in his life threw him out because of his drinking problem, which is how he ended up homeless, which is how he ended up at the zoo.

I had a no-drinking policy in the trailer houses and on the zoo property anywhere because of the way my brother had died. I just wasn't going to support that behavior on the zoo named in his memory. Smoking weed after work was okay by me, but I fired many people for smoking during lunch and coming back stoned.

Erik knew all this. I told him he wasn't allowed to drink on the property, or else he'd be fired, but I'd find dozens of his empty vodka bottles hidden under his trailer house, or anywhere else he thought he could get away with hiding them. I fired him, put him through rehab, and took him back, but it did nothing because he didn't seem to want to change.

We took video one day for Joe Exotic TV of Finlay going to the trailers, and Erik was so drunk he didn't even know who Finlay was when Finlay fired him. Erik was always drunk, and would forget to lock cages and close barriers, letting tigers out loose, which could have led to a real disaster. I was responsible for every family that came to that zoo and expected to be safe; if a kid was killed because of Erik's drunken stupidity, I would be the one to bear the legal and moral burden.

One day, in a hungover daze, Erik lost a finger to an eight-hundred-pound grizzly bear. Just put his hand right in the bear's mouth, like the worst kind of screwup. The bear spit his finger out on the ground.

Another real winner of an employee was "Saff" Saffery, a transgender man from Hawaii with a long list of criminal charges, including fraud. Our camera crew was on hand when Saff had his accident at the zoo, so I'm sure you've seen the aftermath on Netflix, and Saff's missing arm. What I bet they didn't tell you is that the day of the accident, before the helicopter even got Saff to the hospital, I got a call from a reporter at the local newspaper, who told me the accident "wasn't supposed to be that bad."

Was it all a setup? I don't know for sure. But from that day on, there was a cloud over Saff. He wouldn't let anyone pay any medical bills, but somehow they all got paid. Rink had the person who did his legs offer to make Saff an arm; he refused that help also. I didn't know what to make of that, but Saff didn't blame the zoo for the accident, so I had a lot of respect for him. I ignored the strange circumstances surrounding what had happened.

The worst of the worst of my park employees were the studio staff, running the online show and recording the reality show footage. For a year or so, it was all done under the direction of a supposed professional named Rick Kirkham; you know him because he was interviewed extensively for *Tiger King*, probably while wearing that ugly black hat he always had on. He put together a film crew that couldn't stay sober one night of the week.

Rick was always talking about how great a journalist he was and all these credits he had to his name. Before coming to the park, Rick released a documentary about his use of crack cocaine. Despite all that, it seemed clear to me Rick Kirkham was not only a drunk but addicted to pain pills. I put up with it because I figured this is how show business is—if you want to work with creative people, you've got to deal with their fucked-up creative minds. But I started to realize maybe Rick was a little too much of an addict one day when I walked in on him crawling around on the floor of the studio. I asked what he was doing, and he told me Travis had made pot brownies, and he was eating the crumbs he could find on the floor. And here I'm supposed to be the crackhead?

Carole Baskin sent a message to Rick, offering him $20,000 for all the footage from my recording studio. Carole had sent so many similar messages to other employees of the zoo. Quite often she succeeded. But Rick seemed to take his work seriously, and like me, he believed there was a major reality show just waiting to happen based on me and my park. That was worth a lot more than $20,000, he assured me.

Not three weeks later I attended a funeral in Michigan City, Indiana. It was for a man named Randy Lucas, who used to come to my shows at a mall in Michigan City. His dying wish was for me to come to his funeral.

This might seem outlandish to you, but if so, it's because you don't understand the power of these animals. I was doing this kind of stuff all the time through the Animal Miracle Network. I flew out there for the funeral and afterward I took Randy's widow and kids to Red Lobster for dinner. They'd never been to a Red Lobster before because they were too poor to dine at a place like that.

The next morning I had a message from Rink. He was upset, talking about how the recording studio was on fire and it was completely gone. The alligator pits, which were on each side of the studio, had also been destroyed, and seven of our alligators and one crocodile had been boiled alive.

It was a tragic situation, and I got back to the zoo quick as I could. Five of the dead were just babies. The two adults had come from Neverland Ranch. They'd called us to take them in after Michael Jackson died. We'd helped them relocate some giraffes they had on the property, too.

Who would do such a thing? There were a few possibilities. Animal rights activists were threatening violence all the time. That's why the Animal Enterprise Terrorism Act had been created in the first place, because people become truly unhinged in the name of animal rights. As I'd seen with the chinchillas, these people have no problem butchering animals for their cause. But it didn't seem like the alligators had been the target of this crime; they seemed more like collateral damage. It was the film studio that had been burned down. Who would want to destroy that building, and all the video footage?

Strangely, our producer, Rick Kirkham, was nowhere to be found after the crime took place. Rink said he'd packed all his stuff and left the zoo before the fire marshal arrived. When we went through security footage from the gift shop, which faces the road, the camera caught a man walking from the fire to the trailer houses at 3 a.m. When we put the security video online, the whole internet said it was Rick. It appeared to me that this could have been footage of Rick Kirkham, or someone who looked like him. I don't know for sure, but that could explain why he packed and left so quick.

I never heard from Rick again until *Tiger King* came out on Netflix and he tried to claim fame and say I started that fire all the way from Michigan City. Rick Kirkham must be smoking crack. All he is doing is trying to take the heat off himself.

Again, I have not seen *Tiger King*, but people say it makes it look like I burned my studio down. *For what?* First of all, if I were involved, it would also implicate Rink, and whatever you think of me, you mean to tell me Rink was the arsonist? That man is pure-hearted as they come. You're a fool if you think Rink and I burned any animals alive—we'd never do that.

I'm tired of defending myself against these people and their lies. I'm the one who lost everything in the fire, and I'm the one who had to work to replace it all again. Much of the footage that was destroyed was irreplaceable. My whole life was in there; my mom had VHS tapes that we were converting to digital so we could use them in the reality show. There was footage from the pet store days with GW, and early days at the park with Brian. Then I had everything saved from the years two film crews followed my staff around all day every day before Rick Kirkham ever got there.

On top of all that, I had a ton of evidence against Carole Baskin that burned in the studio fire. I had Terry Thompson's autopsy, and all the video footage I had of Terry's place. The fire marshal couldn't find any proof of melted hard drives, so maybe Carole has all the footage that was stolen out of there before it burned.

Rick had been filming for seven months and I owned all that footage, no matter what he says. He was an employee of the zoo, paid five hundred dollars a week plus a place to stay, with utilities, cable TV, all of it. In exchange, he filmed for my music videos, podcast, whatever we had to do, wherever we had to do it. Plenty of other people were doing Rick Kirkham's job before and after he was at the park, and all these people were paid employees, not independent contractors.

It is my belief that Rick Kirkham may have been paid off to burn down the studio, although he has denied any wrongdoing and never been charged for the crime. My YouTube show was building an audience and I was revealing the truth of just what government agencies like the USDA were doing with private corporations like the GFAS. There were well-funded people who wanted to burn down my studio to shut me up. It didn't last long; Michael Sandlin, from Tiger Truck Stop, paid for all the new video and studio equipment for us to get back on the air and fight for people's rights, and we got a bigger and better alligator pit, too.

Nothing ever came of the investigation into the arson. The Garvin County sheriff at the time swore up and down the FBI screwed up the investigation, so maybe, just maybe, the federal conspiracy against me starts all the way back here. From what I heard, one ex–FBI agent involved in Terry's case was killed and it was covered up as a suicide. Imagine that . . .

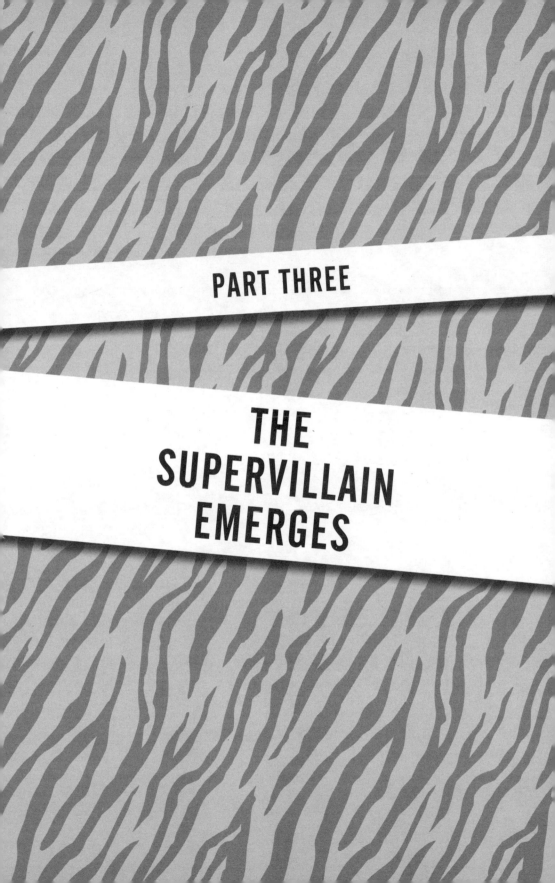

# PART THREE

# THE SUPERVILLAIN EMERGES

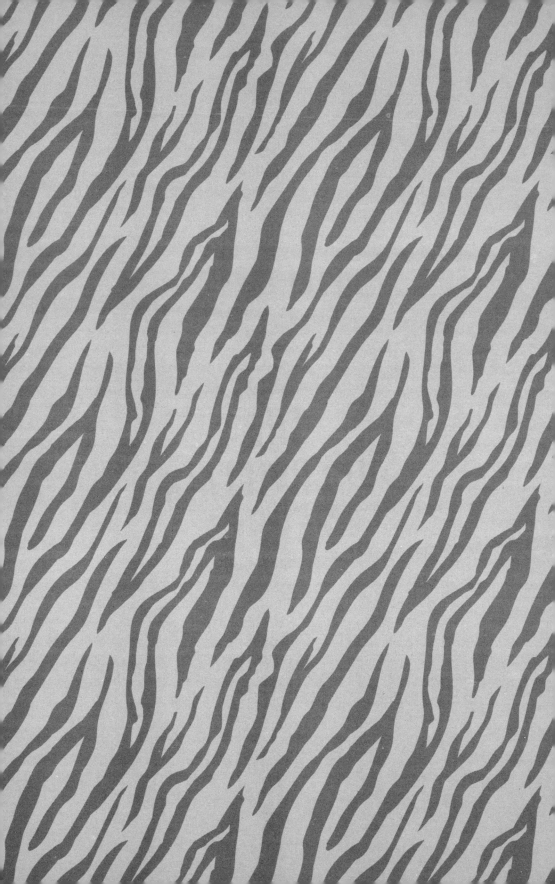

# CHAPTER 18

They say that when a person shows you who they are, you should believe them. That's always been a tough lesson for me to learn. I believe in the rehabilitation of the human soul, which is why I gave so many second chances to so many broken people.

Now, there have been a lot of characters in this book so far, a lot of them up to no good. But of all the ruthless, unscrupulous individuals I've ever met, I have never seen a pair of people seemingly live to scam quite like Jeff Lowe and his slut wife, Lauren.

Sometime in early 2015, this guy named Jeff Lowe came by the park with his then-wife, a woman named Kathy. Jeff looked like Uncle Fester from *The Addams Family*, bald and pudgy, but he seemed nice enough, and Kathy was a sweetheart. They were looking to buy a baby taliger, which I happily sold to them.

I'm sure Jeff really saw something in his future when he came to my park. I had spent the past year posting all about my health problems on Facebook. Walking around with an IV in my arm. "Easy mark" must have been flashing in neon above my head.

Soon after he picked up the taliger, Jeff Lowe hit me up on Facebook, talking about wanting to help me with a fundraiser I was having. He said he was friends with Dan Haggerty, the fellow who played Grizzly Adams on the television show of the same name. Jeff said he could get Dan Haggerty to do an appearance for the fundraiser, for free.

If there's one show I grew up loving and one man I grew up respecting, it was my man Grizzly Adams, who had a bear named Ben. This was back in the days when interacting with animals was a good thing. *Flipper*, *Lassie*, *Mister Ed*, these were the shows I grew up with. Dan Haggerty came down to the park, and he was such a professional and just the nicest guy you ever met. We did a show together for the visitors at the zoo, then he signed some autographs and did some special meet and greets alongside one of our baby grizzly bears.

When it was time for Dan to leave, he asked me who he should talk to about getting paid. I told him to wait right there and I called Jeff and asked what the deal was, since I was told this was a free appearance.

Jeff says to me he ain't paying him because Dan Haggerty wouldn't be anyone without Jeff Lowe, and that, in his version of events, Dan had been drunk on the side of the road when Jeff had found him and made him who he was.

Now I'm thinking, *Jeff Lowe made Grizzly Adams who he was? Yeah, okay.* I hung up the phone and went out and asked Dan what he was due. I paid him, and thanked him for his time.

A few months later, Jeff called again and said he was looking to buy a zoo out in Colorado, and asked me to come check it out with him. It just so happened that Travis and I had gotten legally married a short time before, so I thought, *Hell, let him fly us out there and we can treat it as a honeymoon.* I wanted to take Travis skydiving and there was a great place in Colorado.

Jeff and Kathy picked us up at the airport and took us to their house in Colorado Springs, a mansion with a Ferrari and a Hummer in the driveway, and a full-size pool inside. It looked like the man could afford anything he desired, and to hear him tell it, he was indeed mightily rich. I told him that was a good thing because running a zoo is expensive.

We went to look at the zoo he was wanting to buy and it wasn't bad at all, just had a bad name and the state hated it being there. But it was my expert opinion that there was a lot he could do with it to turn it around and make it a success.

Looking back, I was way too gullible and had no idea I was walking into a trap. But with Travis there I wasn't thinking with my business brain—I was out there celebrating my love. Over the course of the weekend I must have told Jeff my whole life story, and all my troubles, including all about Carole and Howard Baskin, who were still coming after me trying to get their million dollars.

Mediation was supposed to start, and Carole was coming after my assets, which was putting me in a real financial bind. Jeff seemed concerned and interested in my predicament. I admitted to him I wasn't sure how much longer I could keep the park running because Carole's lawyers were bankrupting me. That's Carole's apparent gig, to make you pay attorneys all the way through depositions and discovery, then she drops the suit a week before trial, and sues you again a month later. She does that over and over again until you run out of money. With all the millions she rakes in from donations, she can bankrupt anyone she wants.

That don't mean I was running scared. When me and Travis got back home I released my most popular music video to date, "Here Kitty Kitty," a song about what I believe happened to Don Lewis. I hired a Carole Baskin lookalike and had her reenacting the feeding of human body parts to tigers. Jeff Lowe loved it; he seemed to fully appreciate what I'd been going through.

Come up on Halloween and Jeff asked us to come back to Colorado to attend a big party he was throwing. This time the vibe was a little different because Jeff and Kathy were fighting. Jeff told me a little bit about it, that he'd been trying to bring another woman into the relationship. He wanted to "keep up" with me and Doc Antle, he said.

None of this sounded good to Kathy. The last night we were there, Jeff beat her up and slept on the couch. Me and Travis didn't know what to say, but we clung on to each other even tighter. God, I was so happy to be in a healthy relationship for once.

We left the next morning, as I had to get to Oklahoma City to sit down for mediation with Howard Baskin. Carole wasn't there—it was Howard and me in different rooms, with lawyers running back and forth, trying to come to terms. After about seven hours of that I went to Howard's room and said, "Fuck, we are two grown men, can we sit in one room and work this out?"

So we did. Nothing was said about any of the online stuff; he didn't mention "Here Kitty Kitty" (even though he was commenting negatively on it everywhere it appeared online). What he wanted was for me to stop breeding, stop cub petting, not to post photos of staff and the public with tiger cubs or adults, and to pay $5,000 a month. He agreed to let me work through the summer of

2016 using the cubs to pay all the outstanding bills, and then shut down to the public in the fall of 2016.

It took a total of ten hours but finally we'd come to an agreement. He called Carole to tell her the terms and I could tell right away this greedy bitch was going to ruin it. She said that wasn't enough. She wanted my mom's house as collateral.

I told them to go to hell, the deal was off. Dealing with Howard was a waste of time; he was, it seemed to me, just a big old puppet controlled by a bunch of strings, except it's not strings, it's Carole's pubic hair.

Jeff Lowe called the next day and said his plans for the zoo in Colorado had gone to shit. He said, "You want to sell your zoo?"

I said "No," but since he looked so rich, I said, "How about you come on as an investor?"

He said he'd think about it.

Well, only a couple days later, Jeff got arrested for beating and choking Kathy again. I found out when this girl Lauren calls me up asking to borrow money to get Jeff out of jail. No idea who she was, but I said, "What you calling me for, I'm broke. Jeff's the one who's got the money."

I should have gotten the clue then. I stuck up for the bastard every step of the way. Lauren got Jeff out, and the two of them came to stay with me and Travis at the park. They needed to get out of Colorado, which was understandable, and I agreed to let them move in on a long-term basis. That's when Jeff and I really got to talking about a business arrangement, with him coming on to help me take care of the park.

It was really exciting at the time: he was going to invest money in the zoo to help take it to the next level. I could stay at the park and still oversee things, and keep my animals there, but the burden of keeping things afloat would now be on Jeff. I was fully on board with this arrangement.

During a mediation call with Carole and Howard, Jeff Lowe let them know he wasn't going to be settling anything. "Fuck you, Howard, and fuck your cunt wife."

It seemed like an answer to my prayers, to finally have someone who could really help. Mom and Dad both thought Jeff was honest—I mean, he did put on quite a show. That's how he got us all to agree to put his name on the land, alongside my mom's. We figured that way neither Carole nor my greedy siblings would ever be able to get it. Jeff also talked me into letting him pay my life insurance policy and being half of the beneficiary for it with Travis.

In the beginning of February 2016, I lost another court case to Carole, and I was officially broke. I did what seemed like the only option: I dissolved the zoo and turned it over to Jeff Lowe. It would now officially be called the Greater Wynnewood Exotic Animal Park. Taking GW's name off the zoo was no big thing. It was more about the paperwork than anything else. "GW" was still what people called the zoo. His name remained on the big highway exit signs and I told his story at the opening of every show I did.

I would still be on hand, running the park, but I'd be a silent partner now. I was to be hired and paid $450 a week as the entertainment director, perform two shows a day, and oversee the care of the animals. Jeff would pay all expenses and invest over $500,000 into the zoo. My thinking was, the million owed to Carole was owed by me and my park. Jeff's name was already on the land anyway, so I might as well just turn it over to him. If my park didn't exist, there would be nowhere for Carole to get her money.

Turns out that's a crock of shit and I'd been given some bad legal advice, to let her get a judgment on me. I filed for bankruptcy, ready for it to all go away, but Carole came after me in the bankruptcy court, too.

Jeff couldn't stop talking out his ass on my YouTube show or on Facebook, about how he was paying all my attorney bills now and Carole should bring it on. Except the problem was, he didn't have the money to back up his big mouth. Carole did, and she sued him for illegal transfer of assets, and to this day she is still dragging him through the mud in federal court, spending millions of dollars trying to collect nothing. Jeff denies any wrongdoing.

Once Jeff and Lauren moved to my zoo to live in my house with Travis and me, it took about two months to figure out they were apparently scammers. Jeff, it turned out, had been convicted of fraud for scamming a domestic abuse nonprofit out of over a million dollars in South Carolina. Never spent a day in prison; I believe he blackmailed the right people to get out of there. This is what I think Jeff Lowe is good at: being a con artist and blackmailer. People like Jeff just slide through the system being corrupt.

The big mansion in Colorado? The Ferrari and the Hummer? From what I saw, they weren't his. Turns out Jeff really was just a broke, bald, washed-up old man who had his mind on nothing but sex 24/7.

I also found out the full story of who Lauren was: a stripper Jeff was keeping in South Carolina who he wanted to bring into his marriage. Kathy wasn't going for it, so Jeff left her for Lauren, which is a shame because Kathy really was a good lady, and Lauren is a conniving whore.

I had made a big mistake. Jeff Lowe was an incredibly lazy man; making money using other people is what he specialized in. He didn't plan on working at a zoo, and would be resolving none of my problems. I would never be able to work with him but it was too late. His name was on everything and here I was stuck basically working for a seeming con man at a zoo it took me twenty years to build. But I got news for Jeff: He will never be me. I will die being the Tiger King.

# CHAPTER 19

As soon as Jeff officially took over, here comes his lackey, Allen Glover. Allen came in on a train to Oklahoma with a Weed-wacker in hand, ready to do the mowing and trim the grass around the cages and stuff. Turned out he was basically hired to be Jeff's bitch. If you shaved a set of dog nuts, it would look just like Jeff and Allen standing next to each other.

Allen: a bald drunk who can't string a sentence together because he is always intoxicated, dresses like a slob, teardrop tattoo by one eye, got bad-to-no teeth at all, and you can't get within four feet of talking to him without his repugnant body odor knocking you out.

There are inconsistencies in Allen's testimony at my trial and in his statement under oath to the grand jury as to how he knew Jeff Lowe and for how long. That's not surprising to me. Jeff always bragged to Rink and me about how Allen worked for him in South Carolina and did all Jeff's dirty deeds.

I disliked Allen immediately and did not want him at the park. He was clearly a drunk, and in our line of work that habit is dangerous and destructive.

Just to give you a sense of how big an idiot Allen Glover is: he had a tendency to cut down trees, literally for no reason, without even saying anything to anyone about it. One day, he took it upon himself to chop down bamboo that had been growing for years.

I raised hell with Jeff because that bamboo was a natural shade for the animals, but all it did was piss off Allen. He said I treated him like a little kid, which is exactly fucking right. He was another drunken liability running around my park and handling my animals.

This became one of the first real problems with Jeff and me. He'd let people drink at the park. It caused a major rift because now Jeff was the cool new boss, and I was the asshole always trying to get people to do their jobs.

I guess I was getting on Jeff's nerves, with all my constant complaining. I knew he was talking about me behind my back with my employees. I think he decided to pull a fast one, and took the non-THC CBD oil I was taking for my back pain and switched it out with hash oil. I took three full capsules of it without knowing.

I was in a cage with fourteen tigers when that shit hit me. Right in the middle of a tour with zoo customers. My lips were dry, I couldn't swallow, and I felt like I was stuck in a mirror ball. I finally got my way out of the cage and to the sidewalk and it hit me so hard that I couldn't even find my way through my own zoo. I don't smoke weed or anything, so I thought I was having a stroke or maybe there was something wrong with my brain because I had no clue what was happening.

I radioed Rink (Travis never carried a radio), and I was crying,

I was so scared. Rink got me back to the office and by then I was projectile-vomiting. Jeff walked in laughing, and admitted that he had given me hash oil.

Part of me was relieved because thank God I wasn't having a brain aneurysm. About that time, Travis walked in and Rink told him what Jeff did. I remember Travis lunging at Jeff, yelling, "I should whoop your ass, motherfucker!" I was hallucinating so bad I made them take my gun away until it wore off.

Jeff posted on Facebook calling me a little bitch because I couldn't handle hash oil. He bragged about giving it to me without my knowing. What a fucking mess this was. My employees went from respecting me to seeing me as a laughingstock. Jeff was undermining me so much, I couldn't get anyone to do anything.

After a couple months Jeff brought in a cabin for him and Lauren to live in. It was great to get them out of our space, but now we basically had a sex den in the middle of the zoo. Hell, I didn't have to worry about the tigers stalking the female customers, I had to worry about Jeff and Lauren. We used to always say, "Look, Jeff and Lauren are shark hunting again," because they would lurk back behind the tours we did and scope out who they were going to target and get to go to their cabin that night.

Jeff had a Ferrari parked in the garage, and every day we had a tour group come through, Jeff would pull out that car and start it up, so all the young girls were impressed. Rink and I got so tired of it we put up a wooden privacy fence so tour groups couldn't see the car, and Jeff hit the fucking ceiling when he saw that fence. It was like we'd pulled the plug out of his little game to lure girls home, which is exactly what it was. Rink and I had a good laugh about that one.

Lauren meanwhile was running around the zoo and in town with her shorts so short they'd ride up the crack of her ass. But I give credit where it's due: she was the mastermind behind Jeff's apparent schemes. Always seemingly looking for someone to rip off, sitting online all day long coming up with scams to pull on people. She would hit up girls on Facebook, using the baby tigers as bait, and get them to fly in and stay for a weekend. It all seemed consensual to me at the time.

Many young girls fell for the same scheme, coming to the zoo for work or to spend time with the baby tigers. Jeff and Lauren would come to the zoo office, bragging and showing evidence of what they had done the night before. Most of the crew were sick to their stomachs seeing what Jeff and Lauren were up to. The female employees never felt safe. What could I say? He had his name on everything.

This is what had become of my zoo, after all the people around the world had put money into it to build memorials for their lost loved ones. Travis and I talked a lot about leaving. He hated Jeff so much, just as much as I did. It seemed like the best thing to do might be to take my husband and leave the whole thing behind. I told Rink I wanted to leave and he was pretty shocked. He convinced me I had to stick around to see how this played out with Jeff. In my mind, though, all I had to do was figure out where I could move my animals. I couldn't leave them with Jeff because he had no idea how to take care of them properly. Until I could get my animals sorted, I'd have to just grin and bear it.

# CHAPTER 20

I have always written letters to my politicians, on things I agreed with, disagreed with, or ideas I had. Many were about the animal industry, taxes, Social Security, etc. I was lucky to ever even get a form letter back. They don't give a shit what real people have to say.

Sometime in 2015, I was watching a debate on CNN. Another debate where they never solved anything, just threw around meaningless percentages and statistics. I went to bed pissed off, and woke up the next morning knowing exactly what to do to get them to listen to me. I downloaded the form to run for president and filed it that day. I ran as Joseph Maldonado.

I was off and running, or so I thought. I did not know that an independent candidate did not automatically have access to the ballot; I had to get so many signatures in order to be allowed to run for president.

A good friend of mine named Anne Patrick came on board and worked her ass off to get me access to thirty-seven state ballots. I love Anne, she's got the ugliest service dog in the world, named Bailey, but still he is the most incredible dog. When he gets excited his little corkscrew tail really gets wound up.

I did YouTube videos every day to push my messages, which were pro–Second Amendment, pro–pot legalization, and anti–government overreach. Me and Travis went to Belize and Mexico, so I could learn about foreign affairs. Travis was at home in Belize, living like a native and smoking homegrown ganja, but it was a work trip for me; I actually saw something very interesting in Belize. Belize charges you fifty dollars a month to stay there if you're not a citizen. When I went to Mexico and talked to people, I asked if they would be willing to pay fifty dollars each month to come to America, and get a citizen tax number so they could live, work, and pay taxes until they became legal. Everyone said yes. Why are we not charging 15 million illegals fifty dollars a month instead of putting them in prison, shipping them back, and charging our taxpayers for all of this? Put that money in the bank!

I didn't know what I was getting into, really. I probably learned more in eleven months running for president than I did in twelve years of school. And we didn't do it as a joke; I was very serious about it. I was talking real solutions to real people, as a working American, not a politician. I knew there was no chance I could win, but I was given a hell of a platform to get my message out.

My daily video messages to the public were recorded inside a large arena compound that housed tigers, liligers, and taligers. Most of my hybrids were in there. There was one female liliger, Misty, who was too hyper to do videos, so we'd lock her away until I was done. It required my full attention to speak on video and I couldn't keep an eye on her.

One day I was filming inside the cage, with my film crew and staff watching from outside. Jeff Lowe was there, and Erik Cowie was standing by the door to the cage, but Erik didn't lock Misty out like he was supposed to. I wasn't paying close enough attention. I was standing there filming my piece for the day, and Misty came up to me from behind but I thought it was Itsy, so I didn't think too much of it. Then Misty went straight for my shoe like stink on shit. Bit the end of my left foot and thank God the canine tooth went between my toes and through my shoe. Off we went; she dragged me across the cage and all I could think about was grabbing a post to keep her from dragging me farther. I pulled out my .357 and fired two shots into the ground to make noise so she would let go, and she did.

My leg hurt so bad I couldn't stand up right at first and I had to use my crutch to keep Misty and the others away from me until I could stand. Once I stood up they left me alone and I hopped out of the cage.

Until I watched the video I never knew how close Thor was to the back of my neck while Misty was dragging me. Jeff Lowe, Erik, and the rest of the staff just stood outside the door of the cage and laughed like it was funny that I just about got pulled apart.

One of my employees would later admit on Facebook that he put perfume on my shoe, knowing it would attract the tigers and possibly get me killed. I don't have any proof that it was Jeff Lowe's idea, and he denies it, but Jeff was on my life insurance so if I had died, he'd have done well for himself.

I confronted Jeff about this, and he acted like I was nuts and denied it. He told me all I cared about was my campaign. I wasn't holding up my end of the bargain in running the zoo. It was gaslighting, plain and simple. The campaign didn't take up that much time; what Jeff was probably really upset about was all the attention I was getting. He was jealous.

The night of the presidential election, I was at a libertarian watch party in OKC. I was getting a lot of votes, especially in Colorado, and that night the libertarians asked if I would run for governor. I didn't think I could keep my mouth shut for four more years, so I decided to do it. I changed my party to be a libertarian and signed up to run for governor.

Unlike running for president, running for governor required a lot of my time. For a year and a half they had to put up with me on each and every debate stage. Even if I had slim odds of winning, I still had a major platform from which to share with the world everything that these animal rights organizations were up to.

What did I learn about politics while I was running? It's all rigged and a scam. The voter has no choice who is going to win and the candidate has no chance of winning unless they're part of the team. This was what I'd come to expect because I saw how corrupt government bureaucracies made alliances with private organizations to kneecap people like me, in favor of their friends and supporters. That's how politics works.

You might think I'm crazy, but there is a domestic war on private owners of exotic animals by the United States government. They want to shut down all private owners, and they're willing to do whatever it takes to make that happen.

The tiger market in America is worth billions to Carole, the GFAS, and the AZA. In order to squash their competition, these groups have become experts at seemingly manipulating laws to shut down their competitors. And that's exactly what they did to me, by using the United States Endangered Species Act (ESA).

Let me try to break this down for you. The ESA was created to protect our native animals, within the habitats of the United States, from extinction. They've done a good job at that, a very high success rate. According to the WWF website, the ESA "requires protection for critical habitat areas and the development and implementation of recovery plans for listed species."

Nothing wrong with that, I don't think. The thing is, the ESA as it was designed has nothing at all to do with tigers, lions, or any other endangered animals from foreign countries. A tiger does not have a natural habitat within the United States, nor do I think we plan on creating one for them. So if there is no hope of conservation, why are lions and tigers covered by the ESA?

None of this really affected me until April 2016, when the director of the U.S. Fish & Wildlife Service (FWS), a very rich fellow named Dan Ashe, put up for public debate the addition of "Generic Tigers" to the Endangered Species Act.

This was a very big deal. Generic tigers, a.k.a. crossbred tigers, a.k.a. tiger mutts, weren't included on the ESA, because they don't technically exist in the wild.

Generic tigers were considered by some to be a major loophole in the ESA. It meant that people like me could breed and sell tigers without the same permits we'd need if we were dealing with purebred species. It was illegal to sell animals on the ESA across state lines; that's why all my tigers were crossbred mixes, like Siberian/Bengal. Every transaction for every tiger I ever sold was completely legal.

In the press release, here's what Dan Ashe said about adding generic tigers to the ESA: "Removing the loophole that enabled some tigers to be sold for purposes that do not benefit tigers in the wild will strengthen protections for these magnificent creatures and help reduce the trade in tigers that is so detrimental to wild populations. This will be a positive driver for tiger conservation."

How in the hell does breeding done in America do anything to negatively affect an animal in the wild in Asia or India? Does that make any fucking sense to you? The ESA hurts exotic animals in America: it stops people from breeding them in captivity and selling them all over the United States, which would increase the bloodlines, and reduce inbreeding. The ESA is being used not to protect tigers, but to make them become extinct. Tigers born and bred in the United States are only adding to the total population of endangered species. If we just bred them and sold them more widely, it would ruin any black-market value and they wouldn't be poached at all.

Just like elephant tusks: half a million pounds of tusks were confiscated in Africa, and people like Leonardo DiCaprio made a big deal out of burning it all to keep it from hitting the market. Instead, if they would have taken those tusks and flooded the ivory market with it, they could have ruined the market, and used that money to hire more and better rangers to protect elephants. What a bunch of dumbasses.

This was all about money and power, so you just know Carole was likely tied up in all this generic tiger loophole shit with Dan Ashe. On Big Cat Rescue's website, I saw they were offering to pay people to post comments, so it looked like the public was concerned about generic tigers.

In May 2016, Dan Ashe and Carole got what they wanted: generic tigers were placed on the ESA. People should note that Dan Ashe did well to protect his private business. I didn't mention it earlier, but at the same time Dan was directing the FWS, he was also the CEO and president of the AZA. AZA organizations were exempted from the effects of the legislation Dan Ashe pushed through while running the FWS, thereby giving him and the AZA a monopoly on the tiger business. Dan Ashe resigned from the FWS when Obama left office, but he remains the head of the AZA.

What it boils down to is this: a private organization may have colluded with a government organization to use the ESA as a tool to take out their competition, like me, and create a monopoly. In my mind it's a federal conspiracy. Soon the GFAS and the AZA will be the only ones with tigers, and they are so damn close to pulling this off and controlling who in this country is allowed to own exotic animals and who isn't. They'll keep doing it too, as long as they can imprison everyone who takes a stand. Unless the public starts making their senators and congresspeople answer to what is going on here, activists will continue to write their own laws and Congress will continue to pass them.

If you look at the GFAS website, they wouldn't seem to have any affiliation with Carole Baskin, but I happen to know Carole Baskin created GFAS, with a lady named Fisher. I know the whole story. There is a company called Animal Finders Guide that Carole wanted to be a part of, but the owner wanted nothing to do with her. She started the GFAS seemingly out of spite. When I started calling Carole out, her name and presence were struck from the GFAS website.

This book could change the entire exotic animal sanctuary business by revealing the truth. All you have to do is look up the prices of the houses the CEOs live in versus the cages their animals live in and the amount of assets they have from donated money. I mean, hell, look at Ingrid Newkirk from PETA and Wayne Pacelle from the HSUS. They both are millionaires who I believe allegedly exploit abused animals to bring in donations. Remember, I supplied everyone with baby tigers for fake rescue stories so they could keep up their scams. It's all bullshit; the only animal organizations you should ever donate any money to are your local organizations, including local humane societies (which are different from the HSUS).

Within weeks of the amendment of the generic tiger loophole, Special Agent Matthew Bryant at the FWS opened an investigation on me. I wasn't doing anything wrong; Jeff Lowe was in charge of the zoo, not me. Any tigers sold after Jeff took over the park were his responsibility, so there was nothing to charge me with. I was never the beneficiary of a single illegal tiger sale. That did not sit well with too many people who wanted to take me down. If I wasn't going to do anything to get myself in trouble, they would create a scheme to get me arrested. That is when the conspiracy against me really kicked into high gear.

# CHAPTER 21

Jeff Lowe got my elderly mother to put his name on the zoo land alongside hers, claiming to be this millionaire who was going to invest in the zoo. All the while he had nothing—it was all fake and a seeming fraud to steal the property. But I wasn't the only one Jeff Lowe may have been scamming.

Jeff was always claiming to anyone who would listen that he "made" the career of stunt performer Robbie Knievel, which is weird since Robbie's real claim to fame is being Evel Knievel's son. What did Jeff Lowe have to do with that? Jeff used to bring around a car trailer with Robbie's name and logo on the side, because it made Jeff feel important and garnered the attention he needed. In any photos you will ever see of Jeff, he is dressed just like Robbie Knievel. He needs Robbie's image to be someone—because on his own, he is no one.

Come to find out, Robbie Knievel posted on Facebook calling Jeff a "fraud" and a "loser."

Then there's this guy Joe Barth: Jeff got him to start building a drive-in movie theater on an empty lot of property south of the zoo. Jeff didn't own the land, but lied and said he did. Mysteriously, Joe Barth's house burned down around this time, and the title to his trailer was in there. According to Joe Barth, Jeff knew the title was burned up, so Joe believes Jeff stole the trailer and sold it for $26,000.

Joe Barth sued Jeff in Garvin County and won an $83,000 judgment against him, but Jeff doesn't have any money, so Joe has never collected on it.

Lauren had her own apparent schemes, like she would buy sunglasses online for $10, claim they had once belonged to the singer Prince, and sell them for $500. A guy who worked security for me named Marc Thompson was stupid enough to buy a pair for his wife. I told him they were fake, but Marc's head was so far up Jeff's ass he couldn't see daylight to save himself.

Apparently, Prince had sued Jeff at some point for pulling schemes exactly like the fake sunglasses, so Jeff had Prince's signature from the lawsuit paperwork. When Prince died, Jeff had a little old lady in Wynnewood make clothes that looked like they'd belonged to Prince.

Marc was supposed to be working security at the park, but he may have been jumping right into this seedy business. I'd first met Marc through his wife, Jackie; back in 2014 she came up for my wedding to Finlay and Travis. She gave me this sad story about how she was so miserable because her monkey had died. Since it was my wedding day, I thought I'd be nice and gave her a brown capuchin named George that was tame and would sit in your lap. Problem was, once she took George home it turned out he hated her. Jackie's husband, Marc, brought George back to me, and that's when he and I first met.

We were having so many problems with people breaking into the zoo at that time. Marc bragged to me about being in the service as a sharpshooter and said he wanted to be a cop. I asked if he'd be interested in working security for the zoo, and he jumped at the opportunity.

Marc and Jackie moved up to the zoo and lived in a camper trailer for quite a while, and then Marc ended up sleeping with another of my employees, Melicia, whose boyfriend was a truck driver out of Tulsa or somewhere. Much like Jackie, Melicia was a large, raging, white-trash bitch. Guess Marc had a type.

Marc and Melicia thought they'd fallen in love. Meanwhile I got stuck with the wife, Jackie, in my trailer and couldn't get her to leave. This woman would throw dirty diapers right outside her front door, rather than throwing them in a trash can. Problem was, that trailer was my fucking property, not hers. I had to give her an official thirty-day eviction notice to get her out. Bitch threatened to go talk to Carole Baskin, and then she flooded out my parking lot. When you hear that Jackie Thompson says I offered her or Marc money to kill Carole, that's just her attempt at revenge on me. Go on my YouTube channel and watch how the cops and I served her an eviction notice, and you tell me who you trust, me or that fucking trash. You can even hear her threaten to call Carole on me.

Marc stayed at the zoo and worked on a crew with the animals, helping to build cages and pick up dead cows from the farms, just like everyone else. When I ran for office, he was my limo driver and bodyguard. We all had a concealed license to carry, but with PETA and all the crazies out there, it was good to have him around.

I always thought I could trust Marc. I trusted him to take a bullet for me, if it came to it! That was a bodyguard's job. He went to police school and became a cop in 2017, but continued to work for me, too.

Then something pretty important happened that changed the course of things at the zoo: Jeff hooked on to a big fat whale of a customer who wanted to sponsor a baby tiger. Her name was Cheryl Scott, a single, little old retired schoolteacher who loves tigers. People like Cheryl are the ones who kept my park alive for so long, but in the hands of Jeff Lowe, she never had a chance. She made the mistake of telling Jeff she had $250,000 in her savings account and was "going to make sure that tiger is taken care of."

Jeff and Lauren seemed like hyenas chewing at a half-dead wildebeest. That's when they set up a cub-petting place in an old empty mall in Oklahoma City. They called it Neon Jungle, and it was a waste of money.

The real problem with Neon Jungle was that PETA and Carole Baskin were hell-bent on taking it down, and they came after Jeff, hard. This was around June 2017, and animal welfare investigators were getting reports and doing investigations into Neon Jungle nonstop. Jeff was pissed, really feeling the crunch. Opening his big mouth about Carole and calling her a cunt had only made her target him more, and she was draining him. By the end of summer 2017, Neon Jungle was shut down.

On social media, dumb Carole was posting videos of herself riding on a bike path to work every day, looking like the old lady in the *The Wizard of Oz*, singing, "Hey, all you cool cats and kittens." That gave Jeff an idea. He would sit at his computer in the zoo office, for hours, Google-Earthing Carole's house, saying stuff like, "Man, I could sit right here in this tree and take her out when she rolls up the driveway, or sit in a canoe and paddle across this waterway and no one would ever know it."

Jeff was keeping tabs not only on Carole but also her lawyers. He found an address for a lawyer in OKC—who is still suing Jeff, by the way. He said he was planning on doing something to her, but I didn't think much of it. I joked about killing Carole on my online show almost every day. This was just how we talked, none of what I was doing was serious. There was a blow-up sex doll I'd put Carole's face on, and I shot it up on camera once or twice. I'd take out one of the deadly snakes I had at the zoo and tell my online audience that Carole should be expecting a special delivery. Travis would even joke that he'd go down there and do it. It's a free country and we've got the First Amendment; I was just messing around, I wasn't taking any action toward killing the woman, and as far as I could tell, neither was Jeff Lowe.

Then one day, another consequential little old lady came to town. Lauren had met a girl on Facebook who lived in Las Vegas and who I believe was going to come down to the park to fuck Jeff and Lauren. They went out to the airport to get her, and I was there when she got to the park. This girl was no girl; she was a woman by every definition. Had to be in her late fifties or early sixties, a short little Asian woman.

Man, Jeff and Lauren were pissed. They were planning to party and have sex all night, but it turned out to be an old lady playing her own scam. Ha! Her flight back wasn't for a couple days, so they were stuck with her.

The next morning Jeff and Lauren were on the porch of the zoo office, and Jeff had this book—a hardback, red, diary-type notebook—and inside were well over seventy-five photos, each with a corresponding set of every bodily measurement you would need to know on a woman, alongside a phone number.

"She is into sex trafficking," I recall Jeff saying. "We found this when we went through her bags last night. I am going to tell her she has to cut me in or I am turning her in." In my mind, that's how the man worked. Ripping people off, and using others to get what he wants.

About two hours later the lady came to the porch and Jeff did exactly that. He said to her, "I found this in your stuff last night, and I can give you two options: you can either cut me in or I am calling the cops and turning you in."

The woman was stunned, but she knew she'd been busted so she agreed. The whole day, she was standing around the office, inside and out, on the phone, lining up girls to go to work that night.

The next day she was set to leave for Vegas, but now Jeff and Lauren were going with her.

Jeff pretty much never came back to the park once they went out to Vegas. He rented a house there, started doing private cub pettings. He was sneaking baby tigers into hotel rooms in his luggage, and charging people to come up to his room to play with them. And he was selling them, too. Selling lots of cubs!

He also had a new business idea: a Vegas party bus that would haul tourists around while they played with a baby tiger or lion. A "jungle bus," he called it.

Cheryl, the retired schoolteacher, pretty much bought the bus and paid for the wrap advertisement to go around it. I felt bad—Cheryl thought she was helping tigers. I doubt she expected to be bankrolling Jeff's business ventures. One day I asked Cheryl how deep in debt the zoo was to her, and she wouldn't give me a straight answer. I was just curious, not trying to start any trouble. Jeff texted me a couple hours later to bitch that what he was doing and the money he was borrowing was none of my business.

You know this YouTube star guy, Logan Paul? Jeff sold him a tiger cub. Logan Paul posted a video of the cub with a mean little Pomeranian yapping in its face, and the cub was so scared his rectum came out and was dripping blood. Jeff texted it to me and said, "Shit, this bastard is already in trouble."

Logan Paul got busted and claimed he bought the thing at a flea market. The cub ended up at a teaching zoo in California somewhere. One of Logan Paul's friends or employees got stuck with like a $60,000 fine and three years of probation, I believe. Jeff never got in trouble at all.

With Jeff and Lauren in Vegas, I was left to run the mess he created. None of my employees listened to anything I said anymore. If I gave them a hard time they just called Jeff, or worse, they'd call Carole Baskin. And that is when Allen and I really didn't get along because he would call Daddy Jeff and complain Joe was being mean. My park was no longer mine; I had officially lost all control of my employees.

I had a long talk with my mom about what the hell we were going to do.

"What would GW want you to do?" she asked.

"He'd want me to do whatever it took to be happy. But we worked too hard to throw all this away," I said. Mom and I hugged real tight, and she told me she was proud of me, no matter what. If only I'd known how little time I had left to hug my mother, I don't think I ever would've let her go.

# CHAPTER 22

Ready to meet one more lowlife? James Garretson fits right in with the bunch. I always called James "Chucky" because he's short and creepy looking and pure evil on the inside, just like the killer doll. The first time I ever met James, he was in trouble with lions in Texas, and we had to go get them and board them at our zoo. That was back in the early 2000s. Then I saw him again around 2010 when he sold Rink a stolen Hummer, which James denies. We called the cops on him and he disappeared. Then, in 2016, he met Jeff Lowe and latched on.

James and Jeff were two of the biggest losers I have ever met in my life. They used people and didn't give a shit if it was a young girl or an old lady; as long as they made money out of it, I think they'd take anyone to the cleaners.

From what I saw, James Garretson was up to some shady things. I believe he takes a name with a bad credit score and connects it to a Social Security number and a phone from Walmart. Then he makes it look like the person is making high car payments to get the credit score up, then he gets credit cards in their name for CareCredit, Wayfair, Bowflex, and so on. James would sit in the office on Jeff's computer and may have ordered tens of thousands of dollars of Wayfair and Bowflex merchandise and have it delivered to houses the two of them had supposedly rented using fake names. Jeff would send me screenshots of all this shit, bragging about it, thinking he was impressing me. I'd just save them all, knowing one day they'd probably be evidence in a trial. I still have all those screenshots. The feds were never interested in seeing them.

It seems to me that James is more crooked than you can imagine. Shit, I have $4,000 worth of stolen teeth in my head thanks to that bastard. I had a bad toothache and James said he had a CareCredit card that was about to expire, so I traded him a snow tiger and a white tiger for $4,000 of credit to fix my teeth, and then made similar terms for teeth for a couple of my employees. We all got stolen teeth in our heads, thinking it was James just being nice, but come to find out he allegedly makes these fake accounts using stolen identification and has a shit ton of them.

I had always known that Jeff and James were working together on so much stuff. They enjoyed causing drama by getting you to talk shit about someone and then running back to tell them. One day James was there and I was bitching about Lauren blowing all this money buying shit in Vegas while park staff ate out of the meat truck. I called her a "redheaded cunt," and James recorded it and ran straight to Jeff with it, and that was right when Jeff and Lauren were getting married so he was pissed.

Jeff called me, saying he'd just listened to a recording James had of me calling Lauren a cunt. He threatened to come back to the zoo and file charges for me having $4,000 worth of stolen teeth in my head.

This had me scared shitless. I thought this must have been Jeff's plan all along, to get me to trade dental work for tigers, so he'd have something to blackmail me with. I had never even had a speeding ticket, and now I was worried they would put me in jail. It's my belief that the whole business was a setup from the start. Jeff probably knew he'd be able to blackmail me and everyone else who got new teeth. The motherfucker is so crooked it ain't even funny.

That was the new threat I lived with all the time. I assumed from then on that anything I said to James was being recorded, and as I'd later come to find out, I was right. This is about the time when Jeff and James's plot against me really started coming together.

Now, this next bit of information was unknown to me at the time. In the early fall of 2017, Jeff Lowe and James Garretson met at the Applebee's in Ardmore, Oklahoma. They were seemingly there with a purpose: to devise a plan to shut me up and get me out of the way. I knew way too much about the corrupt shit they were up to and had too much evidence related to their apparent credit card scams. I could give the feds names of veterinary offices that James tried to get to run $19,000 worth of bogus credit card charges. This is all in text messages and private Facebook messages, and I can prove every damn bit of it. That's why James hates me; that's why he had to get me in prison.

Jeff Lowe offered James $100,000 to help get me out of the way. James Garretson admitted to this in front of a judge and jury in my trial. Jeff admitted to this in front of the camera for *Tiger King*.

The US attorney in OKC, the FBI, and the FWS all know this information.

One other person knew all about this: Carole fucking Baskin. Right there at that Applebee's, according to trial testimony, James Garretson called up Carole, and left a voice mail telling her he wanted to help her with her Joe Exotic problem. Apparently, Carole never called him back but instead turned over this information to the feds. (I believe she did in fact call him back and may have been involved in the creation of the setup.) That led directly to James Garretson becoming a confidential informant for the United States government, and secretly recording Jeff Lowe and me.

Those secret recordings went on for some time. You can see the text messages between James and his handler, Special Agent Matthew Bryant from the FWS. You'll also see that there was a one-month pause in their investigation. Agent Bryant wanted to give me time to grieve. Get ready, guys, because in a book full of tragedy you're about to get hit with the saddest one of all.

# CHAPTER 23

Every morning at the zoo, I got up at 6 a.m. First thing, I'd go to town, take breakfast to Mom and Dad's house, and get them cleaned up and in their chairs so they were ready for the caregiver when she arrived. Then I would go open the bar and restaurant at the truck stop and have it open for the staff there by 8 a.m. Yes, you heard right: I'd opened a restaurant and a bar, but I've got too much else to tell you to give it much more space in this book. Let's just say I'd opened it thinking it was something Finlay could run, but he blew it by giving shit away and not caring about the business as much as he cared about making people like him. He was too lazy to ever work, so it ended up being another responsibility I had to take on.

Once the restaurant was ready to open, I would go home and cook breakfast for Travis, and serve him breakfast in bed. That was my special thing I did every day.

After that I would walk the zoo and make sure all the animals were okay, and the zoo was ready to open. We had a staff meeting at 8:45 a.m. every day, and opened the zoo at nine.

During the day I took lunch to Mom and Dad, helped at the restaurant, ran the zoo, did two shows a day for customers, filmed all day, did a live TV show every night at 7 p.m., closed the park at 9 p.m., went to run the restaurant and bar till about one o'clock, then came home and lay in bed, marketing online till I fell asleep with Travis and his white blue heeler, Daisy, between us. Man, was she a jealous dog. If I came too close to him, she would bite me. If I wanted to kiss him good night, Travis had to hold Daisy's mouth shut. That bitch wouldn't even let me cuddle my husband!

It was a grueling and often hard life, but I was happy because I was in love with a man who loved me back.

On October 6, 2017, I went about my morning routine as usual. I had to go into town to have the limo looked at, and when I left, Travis was sitting in a children's blow-up swimming pool in the backyard, playing with Daisy. I took a picture of him, gave him a kiss, and said, "I love you."

An hour later I was at the mechanic's. Erik Cowie called me from the zoo.

"Travis shot himself," he said.

"How bad?" I said.

"He is gone."

"What do you mean 'gone'?"

"Joe, he shot himself in the head and he didn't make it."

I didn't want to believe it. I was praying, praying that this was some kind of sick joke.

A friend rushed me back to the zoo. There was an ambulance, the coroner, and all the sheriff's office people, all in the gift shop.

They wouldn't let me go in; I had to sit outside. The whole time in my head I was convincing myself there was some mistake. Then I saw the EMTs come outside with an empty stretcher. I knew then it was over. He was already dead, and all that was left was for the coroner to come examine him. This was really happening. My husband was dead; he had accidentally shot himself in the head inside my freaking gift shop.

I asked to see him and the police said I couldn't. I was still running for governor, and I got the sitting governor at the time, Mary Fallin, on the phone and told her the sheriff was refusing to allow me to see my husband's body. She in a split-second put a stop to that.

I walked into the gift shop and he was on a stretcher, covered. They unzipped the body bag down to his chest for me, and he was lying there like he was asleep, with tiny little holes on each side of his temple and dried blood that ran from his nose. I rubbed my thumb on his cheek and chin and told him I loved him and would make him proud and gave him a kiss goodbye. His lips were cold already.

The funeral home staff were already there and I gave them directions to cremate him and bring me a lock of his hair and his wedding ring. I helped the funeral man wheel the stretcher to the van. I walked the last step with him, same as I'd done for my brother, same as I'd done for Brian. When I make a promise to love someone till the end, I take it to the end.

That night, I stood in the shower just crying with all my heart. I heard some commotion in the bedroom, and ran on in there to find little Daisy, sitting on the end of the bed howling, *howling* at the ceiling, even though that dog had never howled a day in her life. I sat down and howled with her.

I watched the security footage of Travis's death. One of my campaign employees, Josh Dial, was sitting right there with Travis, and if you watched *Tiger King* you saw his Macaulay Culkin *Home Alone* reaction. Another employee, Jorge, was at the cash register, right on the other side of the wall, and never even flinched when the gun went off. Not one staff member used their training to try to save him. When I saw that, I felt hate in my heart for a lot of my employees.

All Travis's death did for the crew was give them an excuse to get even more drunk, more of the time. The ones who saw him in the gift shop bleeding to death blamed PTSD on all their problems from then on out. Saff seemed to have stolen $1,400 in cash before Travis's body was even taken from the zoo. He was supposed to go to the auction in Missouri to pick up some animals, but he came home with no animals or money, and when Rink asked where the money went, Saff said, "I ain't telling you."

That's when Rink said he wanted nothing more to do with him, and threw Saff out of the park. Saff never accounted for that money.

Part of me wondered if someone messed with his gun. Maybe that is why the cashier never went to see what the gunshot was about. I will never have respect for any of them.

We had the funeral at the zoo a week later. Jeff and Lauren came back from Vegas for it and I was ashamed to even have them there, because Lauren was dressed like a slut like always and they insisted on riding in the limo to and from the funeral home. Travis's mom was so high on meth she got lost at the funeral home and rode a motorcycle back to the zoo with some biker.

As big of a wreck as I was, I held it together enough to even be the pastor at the funeral. Mom and Dad took it pretty hard, though Dad had bad Alzheimer's by that point, so he didn't remember Travis much of the time. Finlay might pretend that he is this big tough guy, but he was crying more at the funeral than anyone. I had to tell him to get it together.

Once the funeral was all over, reality really hit me. I just started crying and couldn't stop. I'd bought the gun that ended Travis's life. The guilt was consuming me. I knew exactly how my dad had felt when my brother died. I'd been through so much, but I didn't think I'd be able to go through this level of grief.

I wanted to eat my gun. If I did it, could I still go be with him? Would God understand why I had to do it?

What's really crazy is that the feds put a pause on their investigation of me at this time. They gave me the month off, according to their texts. If they really thought I was a murderer, who gives a murderer time to mourn? Don't you think that would've been the most dangerous time for Carole, if I really wanted to murder her? Because the day after the funeral I went off the deep end. I sat in the studio that we built onto the house, where Travis spent his days playing games and watching TV. I sat in his chair in there and broke down, took out my gun, and shot the TV, the couch, and anything else around. There was one bullet left. I put the gun to my head and pulled the trigger. Nothing happened. I was too crazed to even realize it.

I sat there so long, when Finlay finally found me, the snot from my nose was hanging out clear to the floor. He took the gun from my hand, picked me up, and set me on my bed. Then he opened the gun up and said, "Fuck, Joe, there is still a live bullet in here that didn't go off." The hammer had dented the primer of the bullet, but the bullet didn't fire.

I should have died that night. By every law of human nature, that should have been the end of Joe Exotic. Something spiritual must have taken over, I know that in my heart; God must not have been done with me.

Finlay stayed there until Amber brought the kids over. They all stayed with me for some time after the funeral. Little baby Kimber's sweet face was the only thing that could keep me alive another day. At night she would bring a bunch of her favorite toys to bed and we'd watch *Paw Patrol* until she fell asleep.

Kimber could see things we couldn't. She saw Travis many times. "Uncle Travis has a boo-boo by a bang bang," she said, and no one had told her he was even dead. On her iPad, she had a photo of her face and behind her, plain as day, was Travis's head.

A lot of people go around saying that Travis wasn't really gay, Joe must've made him live that way. That hurts. Travis and I got legally married and slept together for four years. That's pretty gay. To ignore or turn evil my intentions won't ever change the fact that he fell in love with me. When I met Travis I fell so in love with that man and was so proud of him for getting his life together. He never once was ashamed of saying he was my husband. Unlike Finlay, Travis was in love with me, and I was attractive enough for him. He made me feel good about myself, which hadn't been the case for a long time. Nothing else mattered. Open your eyes and hearts to that fact and enjoy the life Travis had; don't throw dirt on his name in his death.

Those of you who are familiar with loss may already know this, but to those of you blessed with ignorance of it, I give you this advice: Never leave anyone you love without saying "I love you." If you love someone, you must state it confidently, fully, all three words: "I love you." It matters for people who matter. Regardless of how mad you are, last words spoken are forever. I love you, Travis, and I always will.

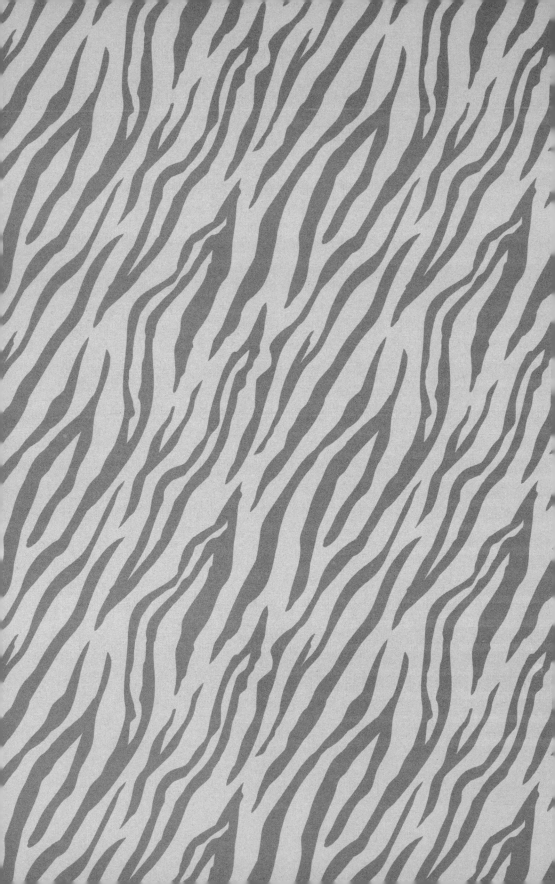

# CHAPTER 24

When Travis died, my soul died. In my life, between human beings and animals, I have seen more death than one person should ever have to witness. It seemed like anything that meant anything to me God took away. All I thought about all day every day was dying. I couldn't go in the gift shop without seeing the hole in the wall, the bare patch cut out of the carpet where he'd died because there had been so much blood. Rink burned the chair Travis had been sitting in, and all the stuff on the desk, too.

I was done, with everything. I quit taking my gun to work with me, hoping a tiger would kill me. I wrote a do-not-resuscitate order (DNR) and kept it under the register so if I got hurt they would have to let me bleed out.

A few days after the funeral, I walked around the park, checking on the animals before we opened. I talked to Travis as I worked, just crying and telling him how much I missed him and how much it hurt he wasn't there. I told him, "I robbed you of almost five years of your life because of this zoo." Everything had to be about the zoo. I was so caught up in the drama instead of enjoying life with the man I loved.

The animals comforted me as I saw them. They all knew something horrible had happened. They were my family. I got to the front of Tiger Alley, where we kept the crippled tigers. I saw my cats that were limping, and three-legged ones, and the ones with no tails because they'd been chewed off. Why was I keeping all these animals alive? Why? Because they bring in donations.

My priorities had changed, I could feel it in my gut, but I wasn't sure what to do. I remember thinking about Travis and I just looked up in the sky and said, "Travis, give me a sign you made it up to Heaven. I don't think I can go on any further if I don't know you're okay."

There, in the sky, I saw it: the word "HI," spelled out in the clouds. Aw, man, how happy that made me; the tears of pure joy that came out of me. Right then and there I promised myself, and I promised Travis, I was not going to do this anymore, to the animals, to myself, to anyone. I had to get the hell out of the zoo.

PETA had taken us to court over possession of nineteen tigers we had picked up from a park in Florida, Dade City's Wild Things. The tigers were technically not supposed to leave Florida, but we went and got them anyway. There was a court date in November, but on the day of, I met with PETA and spoke to one of their lawyers, Brittany Peet, in front of the courthouse. I told her if they could find these tigers a good home, they could have them. When the deal was done I called Jeff out in Vegas and he approved it. "Why would we spend money to fight for a bunch of sick tigers?" he said. The old Joe would have reminded him what the park was supposed to be all about. But that Joe died with Travis; the new Joe was done with it all.

Brittany came with a crew from Colorado to pick up the tigers. She and I spent the day walking around and talking, and shit, man, we hit it off. Brittany was nothing like we all portray each other to be in our fights about animal rights. She was a real human being with real feelings, and she understood the position I was in. I told her all about Travis, his message in the sky, and how much I really did want what was best for the animals. I told her I was having a hard time at the park, that the employees were sloppy and drunk and I was scared someone would get killed in there.

I told Brittany, bottom line, I was thinking of shutting the whole thing down. She told me she thought that was a good idea, and that she'd do anything she could to help make that happen.

That is when I put my five crippled tigers to sleep. I'm not ashamed to say it. I saved those tigers from years of pain. I was done making sick animals stay alive just to put on exhibits for money. It was time to end their suffering.

I had always said that if I quit I would euthanize everything, so they could all rest in peace. The USDA inspectors always told me I had the right to put them down anytime I wanted because I owned them; I just had to do it humanely, and shooting was (and is) considered humane. The five tigers were put down the same as any horse or cow we did on a daily basis, and they were buried with all their body parts out of respect.

Four of the five tigers I put down were in their late teens, and the single male was twenty-three years old, about three times longer than the average lifespan of a tiger in the wild. Two were born at the zoo, some of the very first, and three had come in from other places. All were declawed, yes, because back then my vet declawed. Sometimes there are complications where the brain tells the foot to regrow claws, and they come out the top of their feet, their ankles, and even the lower part of the leg. It's extremely painful— just imagine if a toenail started growing out of your ankle. All five of those tigers had feet that were so bad they limped when they walked, and their legs were deformed from walking wrong.

Nothing about putting them down was to make money or sell body parts. Two of my employees, Erik Cowie and Saff, went on Netflix talking about how I put these animals down just out of the meanness of my heart. They accused me of being greedy and wanting to make room in the cages for more cats. This is a story dreamed up for court and the cameras. I wasn't surprised to hear Erik talking shit about me; he's always been pissed at me for not letting him be a drunk. But despite everything, and even though Saff was always in jail for warrants and a felony charge for bogus loans (the case got dismissed), I rehired him after I believe he stole from us. Travis had liked Saff and would've wanted him to get another chance. Never did I think Saff would end up talking shit about me for money and a little bit of fame. Out of all the people who turned on me, that one really surprised me.

The cats I was supposedly making room for were three cats from a very nice man named Trey Key, who owns the Culpepper Merriweather Circus. I took in three of his cats every year to board until spring. PETA had just helped me move nineteen cats out of the zoo and we were already planning on moving more. There were plenty of open cages for Trey Key's cats. On top of that, we charged Trey $5,000 for the boarding, and he made his check out to Greater Wynnewood Exotic Animal Park. That's not my money, that's Jeff's money, and bank records show it hitting Jeff's bank account. If I shot those tigers out of greed, I must be real stupid, because I was never going to make a single cent off Trey Key.

Erik and Saff worked at the zoo for a number of years and knew how the protocols worked and how animals had to be put down when they were in pain. They said otherwise on *Tiger King* maybe to get back at me or because Jeff Lowe told them to, and both wanted to keep their jobs after I was gone. Putting those cats down was about putting them out of their misery and letting them rest in peace, and it was all done in accordance with USDA regulations. I had to have a veterinary care protocol on a federal form filled out by our vet of record—which I did have—and under that protocol, the method of euthanasia was either by injection or by gunshot. It sounds horrible, but euthanasia by gunshot is much more humane; it is instant. An injection on a tiger takes up to forty-five minutes of seizures and convulsions before they can be given the final lethal injection.

The only "wrong" I did in all of this was putting those tigers down, and it wasn't wrong, because I had every legal right to do what I did, same as any owner of an animal has that right. The prosecutor's office knows this, the judge who oversaw my trial knows this, but they seem to have pretended otherwise. Why? Because they had no evidence of any real crimes against me, and if they couldn't parade around the decapitated skulls of these five tigers, they would never be able to convince a jury to convict me of a murder conspiracy.

It's important that you understand where my mind was at this time period, in the days and weeks after Travis died. Because as devastated as I was, there were people around me who only saw Travis's death as a slight setback in their plans.

Jeff called me about two weeks after the funeral, asking where Allen Glover could get a fake ID, so he could get on a bus and go back to South Carolina. He knew—we both knew—that fake IDs were James Garretson's thing, and I told him as much. Jeff asked me to reach out to James about it, if I was interested in getting Allen off the property.

Allen was no different after Travis died than before—he was the same drunk POS that he always was. I couldn't get him to do anything, and all he did was whine about working for me. Jeff was getting sick of my complaining about him and seemed ready to let him go, so none of this seemed strange to me.

About a week went by and I forgot all about it. Then Jeff called again and asked if I ever got it done and I said no. So he told me to hurry; that he'd get Allen out of my hair because he had to do some classes and shit for court to get his license back. Jeff did say he was thinking about sending Allen on to Florida to "solve a problem," but I thought it might have something to do with the Joe Barth situation, because Joe Barth was suing Jeff in Florida.

I sent Finlay down with Allen to pick up the fake ID. The whole thing seemed a little suspicious, and I told Finlay to watch his back, and to avoid dropping Allen off directly at the location. Jeff and Allen could have been recording the whole thing, and trying to tie me up in some kind of legal drama. I didn't tell Finlay that; I just told him to be careful.

I explained all this about the fake ID when I testified in my trial, and James Garretson corroborated on the stand that Jeff called him asking about the fake ID before I did. Let me be clear:

at that time, killing Carole Baskin was the last thing on my mind because all I wanted to do was kill myself. Amber and Kimber had been living with me since the tragedy, and other than that I had no reason to breathe. And on top of all this shit, I had to pull off my annual Thanksgiving dinner because I knew Travis would be mad if I didn't feed the homeless.

By the first week of November, not even a month since Travis died, Jeff was acting strange about Allen going to Florida. He called the zoo and told me to mail Allen's phone to Vegas, because he wanted it to look like Allen was in Vegas when he went back to South Carolina. I still didn't think he was serious. You've just got to know these guys. They live in a play world in their minds.

Allen kept bitching he couldn't fly back to South Carolina, so eventually Jeff had me give him $3,000 cash, as a loan, so he could get back and take care of whatever it was he needed to do. I took the money out of the register in the gift shop, in full view of the cashier. There was no talk about Carole, or any type of secret plan. It was only to get off the park and get his legal problems fixed.

What I didn't know is that James Garretson had called the feds and warned them Allen Glover was heading to Florida to kill Carole. I am not entirely sure why James did this; I suppose there's a chance that Jeff and Allen really had formulated this plan and that Allen really was supposed to go to Florida, as he has since told a judge and jury. But really I don't think that's true at all. I don't think there was ever any actual plan to kill Carole; I believe James called the feds because it was all part of the setup he'd planned with Jeff Lowe and Carole, back at that Applebee's.

Federal agents were positioned at bus stations in Pauls Valley, Oklahoma, waiting to pick up Allen, as per the information they'd received from James Garretson. Allen never showed up. I didn't even know when or how Allen left the park, until a couple days after he was already gone. My campaign manager, Anne Patrick, had booked him a flight to South Carolina, in his real name, on a plane out of OKC. We went to clean out his trailer and found meth pipes and all kinds of drug paraphernalia. That's when I found out Travis's mother may have been living there with Allen. I wasn't so shocked; I am sure that was all because of the meth issue they both seemingly had. I will always respect Travis's mom for being his mom—he loved her, and from what I am told she is really trying to get her act together and dry out these days. But I never expected her to stoop so low as to stay with Allen Glover.

I was relieved Allen was gone, even though it added more work to my days, as I had to do all the mowing and stuff. But at least his drunk, lazy ass wasn't making my life miserable every day anymore.

On November 16, 2017, the same day the FBI and FWS believed Allen Glover was heading to Florida to kill Carole Baskin, Jeff's house in Vegas was raided. They found illegal tigers, lemurs, liligers, guns, and registered sex offenders in his house.

I believe he must have made some deal to get off and set me up. How else do you explain him getting off with no charges from this raid, while I'm writing this to you, one email at a time, behind bars? Someone make it make sense.

# CHAPTER 25

Through all this, I was still running for governor, showing up for campaign events, and talking to the public as much as I could.

Travis's death got a fair amount of statewide publicity, as tragedies involving good-looking people so often do. I never turned down a chance to talk about Travis, and I don't care if people saw anything wrong about that. The campaign was always about a greater cause, and Travis wouldn't have wanted me to walk away from it.

While running the zoo, grieving the loss of Travis, and filming a documentary, I logged on to the gay hookup site Grindr on my phone, just looking for a friend to talk to. Right after Thanksgiving, I sent a message to this unbelievably handsome man to call or text me, and the next day I got a text saying, "Hey, it's Dillon from Grindr."

We texted for a while, then I called him. He knew who I was from my campaign ads, and he'd heard from the news that Travis had died. I spent over an hour on the phone with him, telling him everything about my illnesses. I wanted to hide nothing. I told him I had a tattoo on my neck for Travis, and he said he could appreciate that.

Dillon and his cousin came up to my restaurant the next night. I watched as they parked their car, and when he walked by the window I said to myself, *He is so handsome. He will be my next husband.* I was in love the minute I saw him.

They had a couple drinks and I took them down to the zoo to play with baby kangaroos in the nursery. Then me and Dillon went to the house, where we spent hours lying on the floor playing with a baby white Bengal tiger cub that I'd named Travis. I told Dillon all about my life, about the zoo and my situation with Jeff. No secrets at all. I learned about his life, too. He was basically homeless, living on a friend's air mattress in Ardmore, Oklahoma, with some bad addictions. Sound familiar? That night he gave me our first kiss.

The next day Dillon came along for a parade in Ardmore that we were filming for the reality show. I talked him into doing the parade with me and warned him about all the cameras. He said he didn't mind and played it off like it was all no big deal, but his big, shit-eating grin gave him away. He was loving it. We picked him up in my limo, and off to the parade we went. Yes, it was a dream come true, just like a real-life Cinderella story.

Afterward, we went by the place he was staying and got his stuff and his dog, Lexlie. I took him home and he moved in.

I always thought Travis had something to do with my meeting Dillon. It happened so fast. I buried Travis on October 14, and met Dillon on November 26. Some people see something ugly about that, but I think somewhere, somehow, Travis knew that I couldn't go on alone. Then like magic, here comes another amazing guy that needed to be rescued from sleeping on an air mattress and from an addiction. Dillon will be the first to say, same as Travis, I saved his life. Too bad Travis ended up passing away anyway. There will never be another Travo.

How is it that such amazing people end up in a place in our society where they're needing to be rescued? It's crazy because Dillon was so smart—I could see that clear as day. I knew he was the one I would spend the rest of my life with, so bet your ass I proposed, like, in the first week. He said, "But I am not in love with you yet."

I said, "You will be."

I was so sure of this that he went with it and said yes.

Mom and Dad accepted Dillon from the day he walked in their house. Dad asked, "Who are you?"

Dillon said, "I am your son's fiancé."

From that day on they loved him like a son.

On December 11, 2017, we got married, and I now carry his last name, right after Travis's: Joseph Maldonado-Passage. They are the two men in my life who made me who I am. I tattooed "Dillon" on the other side of my neck from "Travis," so there was no thought of one being better than the other. They would have been best friends. If there were ever a three-way made in Heaven it would have been Travis, Dillon, and Joe.

Don't think any of this was about sex and his being younger, because it was about three months before we even had sex. After we married we realized he had a rash on his hands, which I thought might be syphilis. I treated him with penicillin myself. Something about giving someone an STD treatment shot in the ass really helps bring clarity to a relationship. This was about being in love.

Yes, you can fall in love without sex. People think my days are all about sex and drugs. Now, I've seen my share, but have participated in very little. I can count on one hand and one finger the people I have had sex with as a consenting adult.

Out of everyone that was ever in my life, Dillon had a gift with animals. He loves animals as much as, if not more than, I do. You could see the connection without words. His dog, Lexlie, was so smart. Daisy (Travis's dog) was attached to Dillon like glue; she never got protective of him like she did with Travis, but she would lie on my side of the bed and just whimper until Dillon would say, "Come here, girl," and that dog went nuts to get to go lie with him.

One day me and Dillon were driving to visit friends in Louisiana with a baby coati, a very cute animal that looks kind of like a hog-nosed raccoon. Dillon was asleep in the passenger side of the truck with that baby on his chest, and they had known each other only a couple hours. God gives certain people this gift.

Sometimes I wondered if Travis took over Dillon's body, because they're so much alike. Same pot habit, same Hot Cheetos, both only ever drank water. The big difference is that Travis never argued, ever, and Dillon loves to argue and he is never wrong, even when he is. They may not be the same person, but I do believe Travis had a lot to do with putting Dillon in my life.

Dillon loved the zoo and all the animals. At one point we had three kangaroos, two lemurs, fifteen baby tigers and lions, and a baby coati in the house, along with Daisy and Lexlie. My life was complete again. I promised him when we got married I would take care of him and show him the world. That boy ain't cheap; I spoiled him and made a high-class husband out of him. All I wanted was to make him happy and make all his dreams come true.

# CHAPTER 26

In the brief time between meeting Dillon and marrying him, I had my one and only encounter with an undercover FBI agent. Unbeknownst to me, federal agents had been investigating Jeff Lowe and me for some time.

Back in February 2017, Jeff and Lauren had flown in a girl named Ashley Webster to the park. When they picked her up she seemed to be as batshit crazy as Carole, so they made her live in one of the trailers instead of in their cabin with them.

According to Ashley, she worked two whole weeks and we became best friends. She also said, in a federal deposition, that I did acid and wanted a three-way with her. Me, want pussy? Now you know she's nuts. Ashley was there maybe a week when Lauren made her leave the zoo, but wouldn't give her a ride to the airport. Then what do you know—a big black stretch limo pulls up out front to pick Ashley up.

Turns out, Ashley had called Carole's phone and left a message claiming I offered her $2,000 to go "do" Carole. How she just happened to have Carole's personal phone number remains unclear. However, Carole forwarded that message to federal agents, and it ended up on the desk of Special Agent Matthew Bryant with the FWS, who just happened to have started compiling a case against me shortly after the "generic tiger loophole" was plugged back in April 2016. This is the same Agent Bryant who James Garretson was now secretly working for.

James was such a pest. He would always bring up the same questions just like he was leading me on to give the answers he wanted. Anytime Jeff called me, I would hear from James the same day. Never failed. I would tell James just enough about what Jeff said to lead them both to believe I didn't realize they were coordinating.

If James would have just stayed at his own zoo instead of setting me up so he and Jeff could take mine, none of this would be happening and I'd be sitting at home with my husband and our dogs right now. With all the proof of the crimes James was apparently involved in, he belongs in here, not me. I believe he was using stolen credit cards for CareCredit while working with the feds, and I can prove that.

Marc Thompson, my old employee who was now a cop, still did security work for me, and would sometimes drive the limo when we went to campaign events. Marc was driving one day and I stuck my head through the divider window and asked him if he could help me get an investigation started on Jeff and James, for the alleged credit card fraud. I told him I could maybe get some information that could ramp up a criminal investigation. Show them two can play that game.

"Yes, I will help you," Marc said.

Like a week before Thanksgiving, James was back at the Carole thing. He called one day and asked if Carole was still fucking with me.

I said, "Yeah, obviously she never stops."

He said, "I know a guy who can take care of it."

He started talking about a hit man, and said he knew someone just out of prison who could take Carole out. I pretended to be interested, to try and get information out of him. However, I already knew James was recording everything I said after what happened with the illegal teeth and him playing Jeff a recording of me calling Lauren a cunt, so I assumed there wasn't really any hit man, and that he and Jeff were trying to set me up. What I didn't know was that the feds were involved the whole time.

For a whole year, James kept trying to get me to meet up with this hit man. I came up with as many excuses as I could. I never had any intention of actually meeting this man, and I never once initiated a conversation with James Garretson about it. He was calling and texting me all the time.

I asked Marc about all this, and he agreed with me that it was probably all a setup of some kind. He told me not to make them any kind of deal or give them anything if I met them. As long as I didn't pay the hit man or arrange for payment, I was okay and could not get in trouble. Marc also told me I should bring up what Jeff had said about Allen's phone being mailed to Vegas. That way if it was a setup, they couldn't pin that on me.

I figured there was a good chance James's hit man wasn't even real, and that he wouldn't show up. But he did, on December 8, 2017, three days before my marriage to Dillon. James brought him to the zoo posing as a guy named Mark. Never told me his last name. This guy Undercover Mark kind of looked like a life-size Chucky doll, too, so he and redheaded James together were a sight to scare the tits off a witch.

I played along during the meeting; we talked about what he was going to do and I talked some crazy shit, same as I did on my YouTube show. But when he asked me for Carole's address, I told him, "You would have to get it from Jeff." Everything he asked, I told him Jeff was the one with the information. If I really wanted to I could have shown him her address, but I didn't want him to have it because I didn't want to be involved.

Undercover Mark asked me about buying a gun to kill Carole with. I wouldn't do it. He asked me to buy a phone for the purposes of this murder plot. I wouldn't do that, either.

When Undercover Mark asked me about money, I told him I would have to sell some cubs because I was broke. Hell, I had cubs at the house during that undercover meeting, but they didn't know that. I had Travis, the baby white tiger, and an orange one, too. If I really wanted to pay to have Carole killed, I could have paid him then and there.

Whatever damaging statements I made to Undercover Mark, it must not have been enough to convict me on, because James kept trying to get me to go one step further, and put some money on the table. For nine more months—nine—Special Agent Bryant pushed James Garretson to push me to pay to have Carole killed.

Every time James called me, I told him the same thing: I'm broke and waiting on cubs. Waiting on cubs was my excuse to not make a deal. I have proof in my text messages that we had cubs born, had babies to play with at the zoo, even sent some to Jeff in Vegas for him to use to do playtimes. There was always money there if I wanted it.

I never had any intention of having Carole killed. My wild mouth made me an easy target for a world-class scam. I knew something was going on, but never did I dream Jeff and his friends had apparently spent the last year setting me up for murder-for-hire, I believe just to get control of the zoo. But they got me the month I was most depressed and wasn't on my toes. That's what landed me here in jail writing all this to you now.

Why was this guy Agent Bryant from FWS working my case anyway, if it was a murder case? You think he's worked many murder cases, or had any idea what he was doing? In all the many texts between James Garretson and Agent Bryant, there is one that I really wish I had known about at the time, but it wasn't until my trial that the information came to light. James had told Agent Bryant that security guard and policeman Marc Thompson said I'd "solicited him to murder Baskin." Agent Bryant texted back that he didn't trust Marc. And why not?

"Got nothing for a crooked cop."

Maybe that was just Agent Bryant's opinion, but I sure wish I'd known.

# PART FOUR

# SACRIFICE

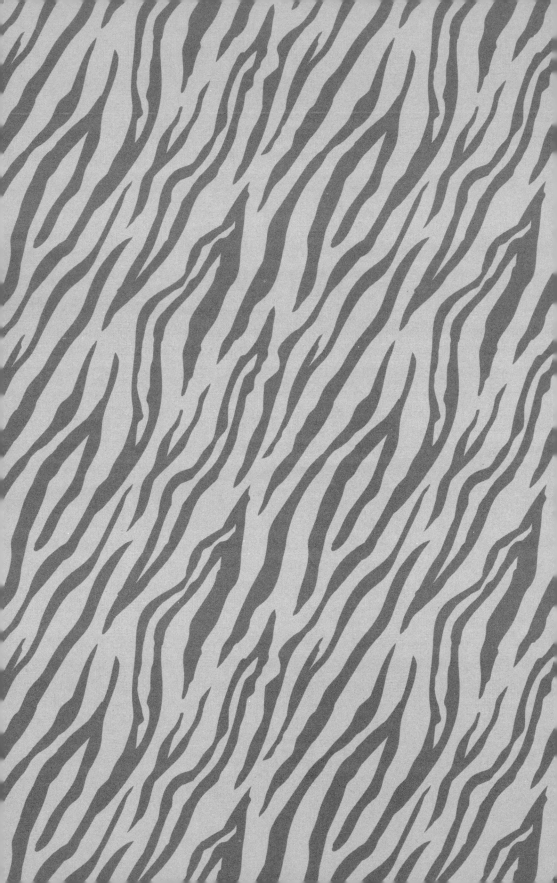

# CHAPTER 27

Most all human casualties with exotic animals seem to me to happen in AZA zoos. That's because they don't allow their staff to interact with the animals. It makes their cats scared of humans, which makes them mean. In contrast, my cats were content and they loved people. They were still just as dangerous, and had to be treated with respect. But they were an active part of a community. By stopping people like me from pulling and bottle-feeding cubs, and stopping human interactions with cubs, the AZA, the GFAS, and goddamn Carole Baskin are making tigers in America *more* dangerous.

There was only one time, in all my years, when an animal escaped from their enclosure at my zoo and had to be put down. It was a female tiger. She was able to jump over her fourteen-foot fence, in the dark. Luckily there was an outside fence, and I found her in between the two, but that fence was only the government-required eight feet tall. If she'd wanted to get over it, it wouldn't have been a problem.

I couldn't risk her jumping over the fence again. Had she gotten out of the zoo and into the public population, it would have been horrific. Not because she would have killed someone, but because the news media would have made a shit show out of a tiger running loose in Wynnewood, Oklahoma. That would give tigers in America a bad name.

Our zoo vet was notified, along with the USDA inspector, and they all decided that the best thing to do was put her down with a gunshot. So that is what happened.

The next day, Jeff and Lauren had all of us in the barn. Jeff had the front feet cut off and pulled her teeth out, apparently so he could bag them and sell them in Vegas. This was illegal and disgusting, but I felt powerless to do anything about it.

And when you think Jeff couldn't get any stupider, he said he wanted to sell hides in Vegas. Selling hides across state lines is a big no-no, a federal crime. I tried to talk him out of it, but he had me send Finlay to meet him in Flagstaff with a new cub and a hide from his cabin. I sent screenshots to Doc Antle to send to the USDA and FBI. I was getting real scared that something bad was coming down. In my mind, Jeff Lowe had no regard for federal law, and my ass was wrapped up in all of it.

One day me and my loyal friend Rink were at Walmart in Pauls Valley when we started hearing screaming on our radios. "The kings are out!" they were yelling.

The kings are two fully grown tigers, King Mosia and King Edwards. That could be very bad news. We jumped in our truck, which luckily was equipped with red lights and sirens (I was also head of the Oklahoma response for animal emergencies) as we had to run a code 3, red lights and sirens blaring, back to the zoo.

The staff were running around aimlessly and customers were still walking around the zoo. Not one protocol these people had been trained to do had been followed. Rink and I ran out to Tiger Alley, and thank God, the kings were in an employee working area. I climbed over the roof of one cage and walked them back into their compound and shut the door.

For every animal—tiger, lion, or anything—that the staff ever let out, I was able to walk right back into their cage without anyone, including the animal, getting hurt. I don't know which of my employees were responsible this time, but I had my guesses. And surely alcohol or drugs were also involved. I lost my shit. I was furious. To hell with these fucking employees—why had I bothered giving so many chances to so many total fuckups? What had it ever given me except broken promises and bed bugs?

I called Brittany Peet from PETA, in tears, which was becoming a regular thing. I must've called her five or six times just crying my eyes out. "Brittany, you got to get me out of here, we got to close down before somebody dies here."

Brittany was such a nice lady, and I could tell she really cared about the animals. Just doing the job she was paid for, but hard work is not so common these days. She came by the zoo again to take a second load of animals away. That's right: one of my biggest rivals for twenty years became my friend to help me escape the hell Jeff Lowe had created for me. I told her a lot of information about the big-cat trade. Twenty more big cats went to Colorado. She also took three bears and a lot of primates. That was just to start; I had plans for all my animals.

I introduced Brittany to Dillon and told her I was eager to get out of the zoo and give my husband a real life. All I wanted was to have a private home with Dillon and some animals. To that end, I asked Brittany if she would help mediate a sale of the zoo to Carole and Howard Baskin. She enthusiastically said yes.

Carole was still suing me, so I couldn't talk to her myself. But through Brittany, we were talking and emailing back and forth on terms. We got to an offer I was happy with: in exchange for the zoo, PETA would fork out $100,000 to help with my mom's debts, and Carole would drop the judgment off of me.

This seemed as good as it could get. The animals would be taken care of, I'd no longer have ties to the zoo—not with its debts or any of its employees—and Jeff could walk away from the financial destruction he'd created for himself. I'd even have some money for me and Dillon to move and get started doing something. Now all I had to do was convince Jeff to take the deal. He was out in Vegas, blowing cash like it was water. I called and told him what I thought was great news. He didn't think it was enough money. He wanted $400,000 to walk away from the park. PETA was never going to pay Jeff Lowe a dime, and Jeff Lowe was never going to walk away from a scam empty-handed. There was no deal made.

They would all have you believe that I was out to get Carole Baskin, but that's just not where my head was at. I was trying to get out of the zoo. I went back to my original plan, to keep shipping animals out, with the help of Brittany Peet, and anyone else I could find. As animals were moved, I'd cut the cages apart so they couldn't be filled back up. These were the cages I'd built with my parents in the wake of GW's death. It had been backbreaking, punishing work. But destroying them was the only way I could leave and be done with all of it.

I did sell some of the animals; that was the only way Dillon and I could afford to leave. None of what I sold were cubs, and most of the animals were given away. I moved some cats to safaris in Broken Arrow. Dillon had a camel that we sent down to Tiger Truck Stop in Louisiana. A primate sanctuary came and got more baboons; a company out of Tulsa came and took lemurs, primates, and coatis; and parrots, alligators, small cats, a large lion, and bats went to Branson, Missouri. All my hybrids and grizzlies went out. A local girl took ten raccoons.

Christmas that year I spent with Dillon, Amber, and her kids at the house. Then, on January 2, 2018, I was on my way to check in on my dad, and ran a stop sign. A truck hit me head-on. I broke my neck, back, and right leg.

As I started drifting back into consciousness, I thought I was having a dream, except it was more a memory. It was me and GW, we were kids, and we were playing with my little dog Onion. That's the dog that got run over so many times but nothing could kill him. He just kept getting up, and always with a lazy-tongued smile. I don't know how he did it, nor did GW, who usually understood most of the strange and unusual things about this world. I woke up smiling in spite of it all, because it was a good memory of my brother. But back to reality: man, I was so scared I'd be back in traction again, like in 1985 when I'd had my wreck. So much had changed since then and yet here I was, totally miserable with my life. Hadn't I sworn to live my life for myself way back then? Hadn't I sworn to myself that I would be happy?

Dillon slept in the ER with me the first two nights. Four days later I was out of the hospital, back at work, wearing a neck and back brace. I had been too busy running around doing everything to pay attention, and none of that had changed just because I'd broken some bones. For the time being, I still had my park to run, and my parents were in and out of the hospital.

There was just no way I could spend any more time away from the park. I was addicted to my work, sure, but I was also aware of the fact that these animals would not be cared for if I wasn't there busting all my employees' asses to do their jobs. Until I could find homes for all my animals, taking time to heal was simply not an option.

# CHAPTER 28

In April 2018, Jeff Lowe was arrested in Las Vegas in connection with the search warrant on his house from November of the previous year. He got a suspended jail sentence and a stay-out-of-trouble order. Since he couldn't stay out of trouble and support himself in Vegas at the same time, he and Lauren skipped town and came back to live at the park. It had been a little over a year since he'd been at the park full-time, and our relationship had soured greatly since then. Things started to get ugly, quick.

Lauren hated Dillon. She was jealous; I was busting my ass every day to work and provide for Dillon and spoil him with a new car and all the frills of having animals. To this day, I must be the provider—that is what was beat into my DNA. It crushes me to think of Dillon having to work or struggle. Lauren just couldn't stand that Dillon had married a loving provider, and she'd married a scum-sucking dirtbag.

Jeff hated Dillon, too, because Dillon was twenty-two and spoiled rotten. I was always buying Dillon shit. I took care of my husband, and Jeff had to be stuck with Lauren and her seeming scams and what I perceived as her wanton lust for sexual gratification from wherever she could find it. Jeff never trusted her; he used to wait until Lauren passed out and would use her own thumb to unlock her phone so he could snoop on everything she did.

We were all ranting and fighting. More than once, Jeff threatened to bulldoze my house if we didn't do things his way. He texted that he was going to "beat the fag" out of Dillon, which seems to me to be a hate-crime-level threat.

To protect myself, I had the combination changed on the safe in our gift shop. Keep in mind, the safe had only guns and animal drugs in it, neither of which Jeff can be around because he's a felon. But when he found out the safe was locked to him, he went ballistic. Probably because his access to ketamine, a cat tranquilizer and well-known date-rape drug, was now cut off.

Jeff came into the zoo office screaming, hollering, punching filing cabinets, throwing papers and files at me. He accused me of stealing money and shit, and selling cubs without him knowing it. He wanted to know where all the missing animals had gone. Then he moved on to his real problem—bitching about the safe combination being changed, and the rant went on and on, accusing me of paying for Dillon's car with zoo money and griping that I bought Dillon so much stuff.

Come to find out Jeff was recording this whole tirade for the feds. He was trying to get me to say I'd sold some of the cubs that I'd in fact donated to safaris. I knew there had to be some good reason he was not in jail, but I had no idea he was working for the feds. Considering what a prolific criminal Jeff seemed to be, I'd never even considered the government would trust him as a witness or informant for anything. What's the word of a man like Jeff Lowe worth? Less than shit.

We couldn't live like this anymore. I called Brittany Peet and asked her to help me move the last of the chimps I had left, which were Joe and Bo. Lilly and Coco had already died by then. Brittany called Patty, a lady at a chimp sanctuary in Florida, and Patty sent her vet and a staff member up to relocate Joe and Bo to Florida. It was sad to see them go and I had no clue where they would live, but I knew they'd be better off than with Jeff, who didn't give a crap about the animals.

I had always kept Joe, Lilly, and Coco together because that is the way they had come. Bo had come from a different place and was much younger, so after Lilly and Coco died, I kept Bo and Joe separated. I have to be honest, I never dreamed that Bo and Joe would be buddies. I thought they would hurt each other. I didn't know enough about chimps to know that most males are gay, or at least bisexual. I wish I would have. It wasn't a week later I got a text picture from Patty, of Joe and Bo hugging each other. I was so excited to see they were together in the same compound and loving on each other just like best friends, and in the same moment I was sad that I had made them live alone all those years at my zoo because I didn't know enough about chimp behavior to know or trust that they would have gotten along.

It's not that I didn't love my chimps, because I did. Lilly was sixty-seven when she died. Joe is about seventy-eight now, if he's still alive. The reason they lived so long was because they got the best diets money could buy. They ate before I did and they had top-notch vet care anytime they needed it. That never replaced Lilly's broken heart from losing all her babies, which is why she died long before Joe. The day I buried Lilly is the day she was really set free. I know I will sit and look in her eyes again.

I should have made my staff go sit in a cage for a day, and see how they felt. They might have spent more time making the animals' lives a bit more enjoyable for all the money they were putting in their pockets off those chimps.

The tension at the zoo became unbearably bad. The drama, the threats—it wasn't worth it. I was ready to leave. I shipped out a few more small animals, and planned on putting down eleven more crippled tigers. That's right, I told you I wasn't messing around; I was ready to put down every crippled tiger living in pain. Jeff threw a fit when he realized what I was going to do, and he threatened to call the news to tell them what I was doing.

In June 2018, Dillon and Jeff got into a physical altercation in the back parking lot of the zoo. I wasn't there, but from what I heard, Jeff called Dillon a fag and punched him, and then Jeff got his ass beat. Dillon knocked him on the ground, kept him down there, and grabbed Jeff's hat off his head.

"He really is a bald-headed bitch," Dillon told me when I got back. We all knew it, but none of us had ever seen him with his hat off before. Never doubt that Dillon can hold his own. Some fags bash back, motherfucker.

As funny as it was to think of Jeff on the ground, humiliated in front of Lauren, this was the last straw to me. Dillon's physical safety was at risk. That was the day Dillon left the zoo.

Myself, Rink, and our vet, Dr. Green, left a week later, after moving more animals. Neither of them could work for Jeff Lowe. To this day, Rink is trying to get his monkey and camel back from

Jeff. As for Bonedigger, the disabled lion Rink loved with all his heart, Jeff ended up killing him after we left.

None of the other staff even talked to me on my last day at the zoo. Jeff had gone around a couple days prior asking them all who their loyalty lay with. Of course they said him, because they needed a job and wanted to stay at the zoo. Everyone still thought Jeff was loaded and would just pass money out like Carole did to get you to turn on someone.

When I left the zoo I walked away from everything my parents and I had built in memory of GW and 151 other people from all over the world. What really hurt was seeing Travis's family side with Jeff. Jeff tore down Travis's memorial at the zoo and wouldn't let his mom have anything from it. Even still, Travis's dad and sisters crawled right up Jeff's ass along with Finlay, Amber, Saff, Erik Cowie, and the rest of them.

Erik was named manager of the big cats; a terrible decision that only an idiot like Jeff could make. While Erik was in charge, the USDA filed a suit against Jeff with over two hundred pages of complaints of animal abuse, including starvation and a dead, half-burned animal in the back pasture covered with tarps. As big-cat manager, Erik would be at fault for all those violations, if substantiated.

The half-burned animal was a taliger named Yi, my firstborn taliger. Erik loved him so much he set him on fire and left him to rot, instead of taking the effort to dig a hole and bury him. That is what I call a hypocrite. The same drunken hypocrite who I've heard Netflix tried to make out to be some big lover of animals.

Since I still had everything in my house, I assumed I'd go back and pack up. Didn't happen; Jeff wouldn't let me back in. Even though he had no legal right to stop me, the sheriff wouldn't stand up to him. While I waited for this red-tape issue to be resolved, Jeff tore the doors off my house and let horses live in it, just to destroy anything I had left and make himself look like a big man. Who the hell lets horses live in a man's house for spite? Wasn't bad enough he got the zoo under seemingly false pretenses and got away with it. If it was anyone else, they would be looking at fraud charges for scamming my mother out of her property and a retired school-teacher out of her life savings, but for some reason the feds have treated Jeff as untouchable.

After some moving around, Dillon and I packed up and moved to Pensacola, the redneck Riviera, on the Florida panhandle. White beaches, clear water . . . what a place to relax. I got a job washing dishes at Peg Leg Pete's on the beach for $10.50 an hour and I was fine with that.

Carole Baskin was a good five hundred miles down the coast. All my problems in Oklahoma were even farther away. Life couldn't be any better than living on the beach with the sexiest man alive.

That lasted a little under a month. On September 7, 2018, I was applying for a second job at the hospital in Gulf Breeze when I was arrested. Five cars surrounded me and US marshals jumped out with guns pointed, screaming, "Get on the ground!"

I was like, *What the fuck is going on?* You would have thought they just caught Ted Bundy or something. Two of them kneeled in the middle of my back so hard I heard something snap. I complied with everything they said to do.

They cuffed me, stood me up, and started searching me. One of the marshals patting me down felt my Prince Albert, and I thought he was going to shoot me right there in the parking lot. He made me undo my pants and show him it was only a ring. You'd think these guys would know about such things by now.

Another marshal was nice enough to let me use my phone to call Dillon to tell him I was arrested. We'd both heard rumors this might happen, so neither of us was totally surprised. They took me to the federal courthouse there in Pensacola, and that's when I found out I was being charged for murder-for-hire. Now *that* was a surprise. What the fuck? I thought maybe the FWS was building a case against me, but I was dumbfounded when they said "murder."

Dillon was at the courthouse, in the back of the courtroom. He mouthed the words "I love you" to me from the other side of the room. There was no way I could kiss or hug the man who meant the world to me. I didn't know it at the time, but that was the last time I would ever see Dillon's face.

My chimp Lilly always told me with her eyes that being ripped from her loved ones was what hurt the most. She missed her babies, and her family. Being ripped from Dillon, I finally understood what she was telling me. I felt like Lilly, caught with nets and traps, taken from the jungle and put in a cage. Completely helpless.

# CHAPTER 29

Though I didn't realize exactly what had happened to me at the time, I'd just been kidnapped by the federal government. They put me in a metal box in the back of a van, chained up around my waist and ankles like a rabid animal, and took me to the Santa Rosa County Jail, to await federal transport.

Santa Rosa is the rathole of all jails. They processed me and put me in a six-by-eight-foot cell with eight other people. One was an old man who couldn't take care of himself, so the other prisoners had to help him eat, bathe, and wipe his ass. Another guy had his jaw smashed from being in a fight when he was arrested. They let him sit there all broken for so long that when he finally saw a doctor, they had to rebreak his jaw and wire it shut.

The ceiling was covered in black mold; the floor with hair, blood, feces, and urine from God knows when. I don't know what it is about human jails and prisons that the care and hygiene standards are so low. Every place I have been would not pass the USDA inspection for a fucking monkey. That is not an exaggeration.

I was initially charged with two bogus counts of murder-for-hire. They charged me for my meeting with Undercover Mark, and separately for allegedly paying Allen Glover to go down to Florida to murder Carole Baskin.

That Applebee's meeting Jeff and James had had back in 2017 sure did pay off for them. I wonder if James was ever paid the $100,000 Jeff promised him to allegedly set me up. There are recorded conversations with Jeff and Allen getting their stories straight on behalf of the US government. You heard it on *Tiger King*: Jeff told Allen exactly what to say in order to get a deal. What I don't understand is what kind of deal the government made with these two known felons, because I believe I have clear evidence of crimes committed by both of them—much more evidence than was ever presented against me.

FWS Agent Bryant told a grand jury that I had received $3,000 from the sale of a cub, and had given that money to Allen Glover to kill Carole Baskin. That's what Allen Glover, Jeff Lowe, and James Garretson all had told Agent Bryant. Problem is, it wasn't true. Nine days after Agent Bryant told this apparent lie to a grand jury, he found out the supposed cub buyer wasn't even in Oklahoma at the time.

The $3,000 I gave Allen came from the zoo, per Jeff Lowe's instructions, as a loan. One of the zoo employees watched me take it out of the register and give it to Allen. There are text messages between Jeff and Allen where Jeff asked for some of his $3,000 back. Their stories never matched up. This whole case revolves around believing the word of Allen, Jeff, and James; and if they seem to have coordinated a lie about where the money came from, how can you believe they didn't coordinate anything else?

Prosecutors tried to get me to take a plea deal, but I refused to plead guilty to this bullshit and wanted a trial. They then reindicted me and added nineteen more animal charges. Agent Bryant went back to the grand jury, now knowing Allen had apparently lied about where the money came from, and failed to tell anyone the truth about Allen's apparent lies. Based on that, I believe Agent Bryant may be guilty of perjury and obstruction, and misleading a grand jury for a false indictment.

Our government punishes you for not just accepting their plea deal. I was charged with twenty-one counts. It's a little complicated, so I'm just going to spell it out for you:

Counts 1 and 2 were the murder-for-hire charges.

Counts 3 through 7 were for "taking" the five tigers, in violation of the ESA, which was stupid because you can't "take" an animal born and bred in a zoo; it is a term meant for endangered animals in the wild. I had a federal permit from the USDA and approved protocols for euthanasia, which included shooting them. The FWS was charging me for something the USDA was fully aware I was doing for years.

Counts 8 through 11 were for selling tiger cubs across state lines, in violation of the ESA. All these charges should have gone to Jeff Lowe, not me, because all these sales took place after 2016, when Jeff owned the zoo. It was his zoo, his bank accounts, so why weren't they his charges?

Counts 12 through 21 were all for falsifying records pertaining to the sale of animals, in violation of the ESA. I wasn't involved in any of this paperwork; it was all handled by Dr. Green and Rink (no charges of wrongdoing were brought against either of them). However, our USDA inspector came into the office on December 17, 2017 (nine days after my meeting with Undercover Mark), and asked me to write "donate" on nine of our transfer forms. Those were the nine I was charged with. She also approved of the euthanasia of the five tigers that same day, all done according to USDA protocol and accounted for in my inventory. We tried to get her to testify at my trial but they couldn't find her, which is weird because she's a government employee, so they must have some idea where she is. If I do get my retrial, that USDA inspector's got some explaining to do, because we have the whole thing on security cameras.

Even if I were guilty of these ESA violations, they all should have been civil charges, not criminal. I am one of the only people to ever be tried for ESA violations in criminal court. I saw exactly what they were doing. They knew they didn't have a case for the murder-for-hire, so they planned to get the jury to hate me by piling on these ESA charges and making me out to be the lowest kind of criminal there is: an animal abuser. I pled not guilty to all these charges and I maintain my innocence to this day.

After a couple weeks in Santa Rosa County Jail, my diesel therapy trip began. They bused and flew me around the whole country, so everyone could get in on the action of charging taxpayers for housing me. I was bused to a penitentiary in Tallahassee, then to this old-ass dungeon of a prison in Atlanta, Georgia, looking straight out of *The Green Mile*. This place had large concrete walls covered in razor wire, as well as mold and algae that would never have been allowed by inspectors at my zoo.

I spent so much of my time in utter disbelief that this was really going on, had been going on in this country the whole time. When I was running for office I'd talked about prison reform, but I had no idea it was like this. I hadn't even been arraigned yet and already I had lost every single one of my rights as an American citizen. How could this have happened?

Atlanta is when shit really started to sink in because it was as close to hell on earth as I could imagine, with humans stuffed in little cells, looking out peepholes, trying to see out. All my senses were overloaded with the smell of burning toilet paper, which inmates used to light cigarettes and drugs. I made it to age fifty-five on the street without ever seeing heroin, K2, Suboxone, or fentanyl. In prison, I have seen many, many people die of drug overdoses. One guess who's selling it. The guards.

Finally I was able to use a phone, and called Dillon. He'd had no idea where I was or whether I was dead or alive. I was so happy to speak to him, but all I could do was say, "I'm sorry," over and over. I promised I'd find some way to take care of him, no matter what. He asked me about getting together money to pay for a lawyer, and I told him not to worry about it. There was no way we'd be able to pay one and keep him from being homeless. I'd get a public defender.

Dillon seemed kind of cold. You'd think he'd have so much to say to me but instead we had the stupidest conversation. The worst part was, he said to me, "I know you, Joe; if you need a prison husband, I will understand."

What the fuck is that supposed to mean? Was he telling me to cheat on him, or was this his way of saying he was going to cheat on me? It set me off crying hysterically. I said, "I would kill myself before I cheated on you." I meant it.

Midmorning the following Tuesday they called my name to fly to Oklahoma. I'm thinking, *Thank God I can finally get to OKC and straighten out this mess.* I didn't even have a lawyer yet. They bused us to the airport in Atlanta where the federal government has DC-10s just to fly prisoners around, each with a picture of the American flag on its tail.

I was off the bus, standing in line waiting, when one of the air policemen hollered at me, "Joe, over here!"

For Chrissake. It was Maddog, a former police and SWAT officer from Wynnewood. He said to me, "No worries, Joe, the truth will come out."

I said, "I fucking hope so," and got back in line. It was humiliating, standing in front of him there in chains, when once we were equals.

This was all too hard to handle. Crazy things started going through my mind as I stood there chained like an animal. Just how bad would it hurt to jump in the engine of this plane? How long would I feel it?

Once the plane took off, I was in the air with at least 250 other people all chained up, and all anyone could talk about was hoping the damn thing crashes. As I flew, innocent, being treated worse than any animal in my zoo, I remembered we had Old Glory flying proud on the tail end of the fucking plane. I felt deep, bottomless shame for what that flag had come to represent.

# CHAPTER 30

As long as I lived in Oklahoma I never knew there was a prison at the Will Rogers World Airport. We landed there and taxied around to a holdover facility surrounded by a bunch of county jail buses. I got on a bus to Grady County Law Enforcement Center in Chickasha.

Now, we are talking about a privately owned jail, a real money-making machine. They pulled me off the bus first, and led me through a garage entrance. I was thinking they were taking me in the back way because of all the press. How fucking wrong was that! They were taking me to a suicide watch unit, because I'd threatened to kill myself in my phone call to Dillon.

I was put in the SHU, a.k.a. the Special Housing Unit, a.k.a. "the hole," alone, butt-naked, with nothing to sleep on but a cold metal shelf covered in dried feces and urine. Food was served to me through a hole in the door, so I had zero interaction with any other person. People who work in jails and prisons like this must have been bullied as a child. They think it's their job to break you.

Their payback to society is to beat down inmates who have no rights to fight back.

If I didn't mean it when I said I'd kill myself on the phone, I damn sure wanted to do it by day three in the SHU. No one checked on me the entire time. After eleven days I was let out, and taken to an isolation unit, where I spent the next year of my life.

Isolation in this redneck county jail is two small cells with a tiny shared room between them. Every two hours, you get to leave your cell to shower, or use the email, phone, video phone, or microwave. There were times when up to eleven Hispanic people would be crammed into one of these cells designed for two people. They were left in there for days with no food or toilet paper either, with only one washrag that they all took turns wiping with. No one gave them any food, so I'd warm flour tortillas in the microwave and slide them under the door for the men to eat. And since they didn't have any cups, I slid them a bag that a pickle had come in from the commissary.

I ended up back in the SHU a couple times, and each time was literal human torture. One time, I knocked on the door and yelled out, "When am I going to be let out of this cold, dirty room?"

Eight guards came in and roughed me up, stripped me naked, tied me to a chair, and left me in a dark, freezing shower room, which was covered in old vomit. They left me in there so long with the straps so tight that the skin came off my wrists. I still have the physical scars to prove it.

I couldn't take it anymore; the mental and physical torture were too much. I was fed up with life, game over, lights out. Since getting to prison, I'd started working on a plan B, and now that I was at my breaking point, it was time to put plan B in motion.

I called Dillon, knowing it would be the last time I'd hear his voice. He was in a bad mood, angry that he didn't have a car and couldn't get around. He said, "Love you," and hung up. I wanted our last conversation to be perfect, but I wasn't even able to get a full "I love you" out of him.

In my cell I had an unopened bag of corn chips. At least it looked that way. I'd learned to open it with a pencil so the guards couldn't tell it had been opened. This is where I'd stashed my pills every day for four weeks. One hundred and three pills. I started swallowing them, and there was no turning back because if I called for help, I'd go back in the hole. Not an option.

As the last handful of pills went down, I felt at peace with my decision. I would never see Dillon again but at least I would live in his heart, just as Travis lives in mine. I lay on my bunk, asking God to forgive me for all my sins, including this one. I don't even remember falling asleep.

Halfway through the night, my body reacted to the pills and I involuntarily threw them up, falling to the floor, wobbling back and forth like a fish out of water. I'd banged my head on the way down and was bleeding bad. Another inmate found me lying in vomit and blood and called for help. I remember thinking, *Fuck, I'm still alive. Is there no end to this?*

No wonder my life is fucked-up. I can't even kill myself right. The guards took me to medical, and they had no clue what had happened. I was given something for nausea and taken back to my cell. Wasn't even given a Band-Aid.

Most of the pills I took were nerve pills, so I couldn't move my arms and legs for three days. All I could do was puke in my dirty sheets. When I could finally move again, I got up and called Dillon.

He seemed to be in good spirits. Before we hung up, I asked him if he loved me. He said, "Joe, you know I love you."

I don't know if he realizes it or not, but I married Dillon to give him a life of dreams. His dreams, not mine. All I could do was pray he allowed me to make his dreams come true. Whether that was building our own zoo from the ground up or owning a house on the beach. Either way, I had movie deals to sell. This book to publish. And when this is over, speaking engagements. If I really want to help Dillon, I have to get out of here, so I need to stay alive and prove my case in court. And if I'm not able to do that, I'll have to find better drugs to kill myself with.

# CHAPTER 31

started writing this book, by hand, in December 2018, four months before my trial started. I wasn't allowed to have any phone calls; I had no way to research my case; and I met with my public defenders, Bill and Kyle, only three times. I can assure you we didn't sit down and go through any discovery evidence to fight my case. We did listen to the recording of my meeting with Undercover Mark and James Garretson. It seemed to me that old James was out to get me all along, setting me up with the feds. I thought in the recording it was obvious I was fishing for evidence, and of course I never paid their hit man so none of this should've come to trial. But I also realized there were a lot of confusing things I'd need to explain to a jury.

I told my lawyers these charges were mightily complex but I was ready to lay it all out for them. "It all starts back in 2016, with the ESA, and the closing of the generic tiger loophole—"

Bill stopped me. It seemed to me they didn't want to learn what the ESA was, they didn't want to learn anything. Bill kept saying,

"We're going to do this my way." This was my life, but I seemed to have no say in my own defense. He refused to call any of the witnesses I wanted, including Rink, who was eager and willing. I felt helpless, so I just started writing down all the things the jury should know but would probably never hear.

The day before my trial, I got to speak to Dillon. He'd gone down to New Orleans for a rave. I had to send him $200, but this was his one time to rave and have fun, so what the hell. I loved that man so much and worried about him a lot. He has no idea how to save money and has gotten too many DUIs. He doesn't know how easily he could end up in here.

I'm sure you're dying to find out how the trial went. The first day was a real mess. One big circle jerk. The federal government couldn't keep its laws straight, and they were more than willing to let their witnesses lie under oath.

Two of the charges against me were dropped on the first day of the trial. Why? They related to a $6,000 payment from a sanctuary in California, for the sale of two lions. Problem was, the check had been made out to my former employee, Marc Thompson. If the prosecutors had to explain who Marc Thompson was, the alleged "crooked cop," their entire case would fall apart. Better they just remove those charges altogether.

A federal agent, two assistant US attorneys, and two FBI agents all knew that Marc was cashing checks for Jeff to sell lions and hide the sale and launder money. They didn't care; all that mattered was getting me in jail. The fact that I had been in touch with Officer Marc Thompson about the murder-for-hire charges never came up in my trial.

My trial started on March 25, 2019. It went on for seven days.

When that first day began, I had faith in the justice system. I believed that as long as I could testify and tell the truth and let twelve jurors hear my side, they would understand what I was saying. But then I saw how our government lies to put someone in prison.

So many people may have committed perjury in order to set me up. Some may have seemed insignificant, like when Lauren Lowe got on the stand and said Jeff paid me $80,000 for the zoo and that I had AIDS. Or when Erik Cowie testified about how much money he made at the zoo to make it seem like I was a Scrooge. But if someone may have lied on the stand about something so easy to disprove, how can anything else they testify about be taken at face value? It didn't matter—none of the liars were ever confronted on the stand about their lies. When Allen Glover took the stand, I was shocked by how well orchestrated his confession was. He said I gave him a burner phone to take to Florida. Said I took screenshots of computer images of Carole and gave it to him, so he wouldn't kill the wrong person. Thing is, the so-called burner phone Allen had was one he seemed to have stolen from my pizza restaurant. The feds knew it was the pizza phone he had. Why in the world would I give him the phone connected to my pizza business to take to Florida? It makes no sense.

Prosecutors knew Allen was apparently lying about that phone, but they didn't care. The phone records for the pizza phone would have shown that I reported it stolen and shut it off. There's a text message from me to Jeff Lowe in December 2017, telling him I thought Allen had stolen the pizza phone. And there are text messages from Travis's mother to Allen Glover, telling him that I knew he'd stolen the pizza phone.

Shit, man, the prosecutors claimed I told Allen Glover to buy his own airplane ticket so it wouldn't look like the park was involved. His airline ticket had been bought and paid for by the park! One of my employees did it for him. That receipt was in the courtroom too, but the judge put a protection order on all that evidence, and the jury was never shown any of that.

Carole Baskin also seems to have lied about a few things. She had somehow, some way been allowed to sit in on the whole trial, so she had a lot of information to work with. She said she had no idea about the deal Brittany Peet was facilitating between us and PETA after Travis died, then backtracked and admitted she knew about it. She said she sued me because I was putting pictures of her face on "lewd photographs," which was a lie; she sued me over the picture of her employees with dead rabbits. She was a big old drama queen on the stand, running through every mean thing I'd ever said about her on Facebook, talking about how scared for her life she was. She would've said whatever she had to say to get me locked up and steal my life, just like I think she stole Don Lewis's life. PS: The judge would not allow anyone to say anything about Don Lewis's disappearance during the trial. I guess if your star witness was a suspect in a murder, it might be prejudicial to a jury.

When James Garretson waddled up to the stand, my lawyer started to ask him about using stolen credit cards, and the prosecutor got the judge to stop that questioning. Why? Doesn't the jury have a right to know how trustworthy a witness is? This whole case revolves around whether you believe the story put together by Jeff, James, and Allen—or if you believe me.

What really shocked me was seeing all the text messages between James Garretson and Agent Bryant in the discovery material. For over a year these guys seemed to go to great lengths to do anything they had to do in order to set me up. They were on a fishing expedition and I never took the bait. Back when I was a cop this might have been called entrapment, but the feds play by a whole different set of rules. I never, *ever*, initiated a conversation with James Garretson. An FBI agent who testified said that after they realized I wasn't going to hire James's hit man, they knew they had no case. So they went to talk to Jeff Lowe to get his story. You know how that turned out already.

Erik Cowie testified that the five tigers I'd put down were healthy. That's not true. He testified that I'd tranquilized four of the tigers before shooting them, which is also not true. I wanted my lawyers to explain to the jury how inhumane it was to sedate and inject a tiger, versus an instantaneous death by gunshot. They wouldn't let me.

Investigators dug up the corpses of the five tigers I had put down, cut off their heads, and presented them to the jury. It was disgusting. They had a veterinary pathologist testify about nothing but the bullet holes, and state that the heads were all from perfectly healthy tigers.

How can a vet make an assumption about the health of a tiger without seeing the whole body? If they had bothered to dig up the whole bodies, that vet would have seen the tigers' legs were deformed from being declawed. Those tiger heads were dug up and paraded in front of the jury only to get them to hate me. It worked. Each day as I sat in court and watched this, there was no one there to support me. Dillon was too embarrassed by the media spectacle, and Jeff Lowe had turned all my friends against me. The only person who showed up was Rink, and I begged my lawyers to let him testify, because if Rink could talk to this jury, they'd understand what had happened here. Rink could tell the jury that he was the one who'd filled out the faulty "donate" forms, not me. I was being charged for crimes he'd readily admitted to! My lawyers did not care. They refused to call him up. The only witness I had testify in my defense was Brittany Peet from PETA. Why won't anyone with the Department of Justice listen to what John Reinke has to say? One of the best men in the world.

For seven days I sat in the courtroom, listening to lie after lie, while, it seemed to me, my public defenders did nothing to back up my story. I was all by myself. The jury found me guilty on all counts, which was complete bullshit. This weren't no jury of my peers—my peers would be zoo owners, or at least ranchers. None of those twelve jurors knew nothing about putting animals to sleep or how the exotic animal business works.

The judge for my civil suits with Carole was also my trial judge and my sentencing judge. I don't know if he's a homophobe or what, but I believe he's always had it out for me. On January 22, 2020, I was sentenced to twenty-two years: a death sentence for someone my age with the illnesses I have. The judge made it a point to say he would make sure I'm never around animals the rest of my life.

My sentence was so absurd, it was all I could do to keep from just standing there and laughing in the judge's face. What a fool he was, and what a disgrace to the justice system. I could have killed three people and got less time in state court. Judges are paid to be strict, not sympathetic, which is why half the people in prison should be let out.

The prosecutor on my case, Amanda Greene, who you met watching *Tiger King*, was soon after promoted to magistrate judge.

It may even be that my public defenders made some kind of deal with Amanda Greene to hang me out to dry so she could become a judge, although I have no proof of that.

Federal agents and attorneys lie so they can build a résumé for their career. This is really how our government and the DOJ work. They don't look for the truth; they don't care if every one of their witnesses lies under oath; they don't care if they send an innocent person to prison. The perjury is just accepted and everyone I talk to says, "Well, that's the system."

Because our system is fucked, I went two and a half years of my life without ever seeing the sun. Imagine that. There are people I've met in prison, things I've seen, that the world would never know about if not for this book, but my story is not dissimilar from many other people's. When you're locked up it's hard to get anyone to care because you're not out there in the real world. The federal agents, the prosecutor, and the judge involved in my case all thought they were shutting me up for good. What none of them realized was how famous I was about to become. Three months after they locked me up and threw away the key, *Tiger King* premiered on Netflix and I was suddenly a household name to over sixty million people.

Five days after *Tiger King* aired, I was moved to the Federal Medical Center in Forth Worth, Texas. As the enormity of the show became clear, the prison warden had me kept under isolation and cut off from normal modes of communication with the outside world. I have a right to communicate with news media but none of my letters or emails to media sources make it out of here. All my calls and meetings with my lawyers have been watched and listened to by guards. They say it's for my protection, but really they don't want me telling my story because they know once the public finds out what happened to me, it's going to have repercussions on the entire system.

Nothing about *Tiger King* sits right with me. It started filming in 2017, with codirectors Eric Goode and Rebecca Chaiklin from Goode Productions. These two seemed to have had an agenda to stop exotic animal ownership, and they wanted to make me out to be some meth-head crazy psycho. Rebecca constantly asked me questions about meth. Now that you've read my book you know I've been honest about my past drug use, but it was way in the past. No way I could do all the things I did—run the zoo, run a campaign, run the restaurant, take care of my family—if I was on meth. And again, tigers can smell that shit through your pores. That's probably why all my tigers hated Jeff, Lauren, and Allen.

Many film crews had come and gone while I ran the zoo, so there was nothing too different at the time with Eric and Rebecca. But shortly after I moved off the zoo, people involved in the show pressured me to let them film me in an OKC hotel room. A good friend of mine was there and witnessed all this. I had no income at the time and they knew I couldn't turn down the $1,300 they'd offered me. In return, they wanted to film a scripted scene of me talking about having sex with Travis as if he were still alive. They filmed me getting undressed and then pressured me into lying on the bed in my underwear while one of the producers took his shirt off, lay next to me, and kissed me on the cheek.

Once I was in prison, the producers moved on to my husband and did the same thing. They paid Dillon to film him in his underwear on the hood of a car under a powered windmill. Then in January 2019, Dillon was arrested for a DUI, and the next month,

Goode Productions went down to meet with him in Tampa and I believe he sold them my computer hard drives with all my information and evidence on it. They wouldn't give any of it back when we needed it for my trial.

Pretty low morals for a film production, if you ask me.

The only good thing to come out of *Tiger King* is that it gave me a platform so the whole world can hear about what was done to me. Problem is, I'm worth more money to these people behind bars, where they can claim ownership of my YouTube material and continue to make money off my name and likeness, and I can't do anything to stop them.

Everyone is fighting over who is going to be in the spotlight for *Tiger King* season 2, but nothing is about the truth. Eric and Rebecca had to pay all my former loser employees to talk shit about me, and now they've found themselves working with so many shady people they are having a hard time making anything good. I damn sure don't want anything to do with *Tiger King 2*.

# CHAPTER 32

J ail is a strange place. It's not that full of crazy killers—it's mostly people who just made a mistake and want to go home and be a better person. Not many in here have done worse than any guard working here; they just got caught.

No one in prison can survive on the food we're given. Food marked "GRADE E, NOT FOR HUMAN CONSUMPTION," is served in such small portions, fully grown men crawl around on their hands and knees by the door where old food trays are left, eating out of them like stray dogs. For ten months during the COVID-19 pandemic, we got two packages of dry corn flakes and powdered milk in the morning, and in the afternoon a cold bologna sandwich, with an apple and a cookie in a brown paper bag. That's what we had to survive on every day.

If it weren't for what little bit of commissary I can buy, I wouldn't have enough protein to survive. I went from 185 pounds to 131. They just did my blood test last week, and it came back that I was low on thiamine, vitamin C, and folic acid.

One thing I ask everyone on the outside to do is go online and watch a video from News 9 out of Oklahoma City about a kid named Justin Thao, who died in Grady County jail. He was beaten, shot with three Tasers, and locked in the SHU. Justin screamed so loud, begging to get out. The guards told him to shut up or he'd never get out. Then there was silence. An hour and a half later someone finally checked on him and Justin was dead. He'd hung himself with a towel that was given to him against protocol.

Go check out the story of the UFC's Andy "the Hammer" Anderson. He got sentenced to thirty years for ghost dope, meaning he never even was caught with dope, they just charged him with assumed crimes from tapping his phone. Most the people in here did nothing more than talking shit on a cell phone. They've been kidnapped in America, just like me. If I end up dying in here, I hope this book still finds its way out so the public knows about Justin and Andy.

I think a lot about all the things I've done and haven't done. On the outside, I always put business first and enjoyed life last. One thing I think about all the time is that I'll never get the chance to swim with an orca whale. That was always a dream of mine, ever since seeing my favorite movie, *Free Willy*.

I'll never turn on a TV, or watch reruns of *Touched by an Angel*. I'll never eat another steak, or lobster, or an ice cube. I'll never play with a cat, dog, or any other animal. I'll never kiss Dillon again.

After I went away, my family fell apart. My niece, Chealsi, got ahold of my parents' house, and my dad was thrown into a nursing home. GW always swore that would never happen to our parents. Both my parents died since I've been in here, Mom five months after my trial, and Dad three months later. They both died alone.

After everything we'd been through, I wasn't able to go to either of their funerals. I wasn't even able to say goodbye; I had no closure at all. GW would be so mad at me for letting that happen to them. I can't imagine the conversation he and Mom and Dad are having right now.

You know, looking back, I have lived the life of four or five people. Hell, I got to grow up in the mountains, work in a nursing home at fifteen years old, become an EMT at seventeen years old, a police chief at nineteen, own a pet store, manage a gay nightclub, build a zoo, be married to Brian for sixteen years, travel the United States doing magic, fall in love and marry Travis, make it through both of them passing away, meet and marry Dillon, walk among up to twenty tigers at a time, become best friends with a chimpanzee, run for president, run for Oklahoma governor, grant wishes for all kinds of terminally ill people of all ages, and all the small stuff in between. All of that so I could say I've done enough.

Now I have to find out why I'm on this path I'm on. There has to be a reason this is happening because this is such a waste of life. God must have a reason if I made it through that much.

Everyone, including myself, thinks, *This could never happen to me.* I used to think people deserved to be in jail, but let me free you from that misassumption. When you hear about someone doing hard time in jail, you must realize that "There but for the grace of God go I." With people I have met, all it takes is one mistake. You have a wreck while high or drunk, or just a real accident with the wrong cops. Suddenly here you are. It can and will happen to anyone.

I guess when it's a big business there is no such thing as a mistake in life. A privately owned jail is housing over four hundred federal inmates a day at the rate of sixty-four dollars per inmate. You do the math and tell me what this place makes a month, on top of the phone and internet charges, and on top of the markups they put on commissary items. Our federal government is paying private jails and prisons handsomely to treat humans worse than animals.

I wrote a letter to President Donald Trump asking for a pardon because of the perjury in my trial. News 9 with Sylvia Corkill out of OKC ran the story, and the pardon thing started getting national media attention. A reporter asked Trump if he was going to pardon the Tiger King and Trump hee-hawed around it, causing the world to go mad thinking he might actually pardon me.

Now that I was famous I had a lot more options for lawyers, and my old campaign manager, Anne Patrick, was able to put together a team of lawyers and investigators to head up my appeal and my pardon application. Led by Francisco Hernandez and Jeff Hoover out of Dallas–Forth Worth, and Brandon Sample of Vermont, they became known as Team Tiger, and they've worked hard for almost two years now to see that justice prevails.

January 19, 2021, Trump released the list of pardons and I was left off, looking like a dumbass. Trump pardoned all his lawyer friends and anyone who broke the law to cover up the shit he'd done, and then pardoned Lil Wayne and Kodak Black. Word has it I should have written a big check and I would have gotten that pardon, too. The federal justice system is built to incarcerate people who can't afford to defend themselves.

In July of 2021, Team Tiger finally got some results. My sentence was overturned, because those prosecutors never should have sentenced me for two murder-for-hire charges to begin with.

As of this writing, I am awaiting new sentencing, soon to be followed by a new trial. If things move fast enough, there's a chance I'll be going home.

Until God sees fit for that to happen, Francisco Hernandez and Jeff Hoover make sure I get everything I need and that my complex medical care is handled correctly. I don't hold out too much hope that I'll live through this. I've now been diagnosed with prostate cancer. I have a large tumor on my right side just below my ribs that they want to biopsy. I tested positive for Hepatitis A from being in Grady County Jail—so dirty with dried feces and urine all over the cell I was made to live in. And I refused treatment for tuberculosis just a couple months ago. I spend more time at the hospital than my doctors do.

Now that I'm fighting all of this, the light's starting to shine at the end of the tunnel. Jeff Lowe had his new zoo raided by the feds, and afterward he reached out to my attorney. Indictments are the next thing coming for Jeff, and he needs a real lawyer to try to defend Lauren and him before they get to experience what my life has been like the last three years. We came to somewhat of an agreement in order for my attorney to represent them and to join in on a RICO suit for conspiracy against the government. My lawyer now has Jeff's cell phone, as well as those of Allen and James, which contain proof the government set this whole thing up.

They treat me okay here in DFW. There's a lot of prison politics. The staff gets tired of the mail—the thousands of letters I get from people of all ages, races, and styles, offering support and some looking for support. I answer every one of them. We are all people who want the same thing. To be loved. To get along. And to support one another.

Dillon never really gave a rat's ass about me after I went away. He let all the *Tiger King* fame get to his head—he had a manager and a lawyer way too quick, and even made plans to start an Only-Fans page, but he's never managed to come see me. No one would even know who he is if it weren't for me, but he doesn't care. We talked every day, but Dillon made it clear he is moving on, and we are now in the midst of a divorce. If or when I do get out, I'll have nothing left to return to in the world, not even a place to call home.

I have met some pretty good people since I have been here. John Graham is the most special person I have met in here; he and I spent every minute of the day together until he went to the SHU. Some of the guys started rumors of me and John having sex, which is untrue, but do we care about each other? You bet your ass. John always says to me, "We need to get you healthy so you can go home." He treats me with more respect and concern than Dillon ever thought of. John has a son that just turned sixteen, and all we talk about is both of us getting out, picking up his son, and the three of us together going on the world tour I have been offered. I hope they allow John to stay on this compound when he finishes his punishment for what he did wrong to get put in the SHU.

In 2021, Carole started going around saying she would support a pardon for me, if I would support her Big Cat Public Safety Act. This woman really has some nerve. She did everything she could on the witness stand to act like she was in fear for her life so she could put me in prison, for supposedly trying to kill her. And now she's out there saying she'll help me get free, if I'll only promote her ban? Shouldn't that tell you everything you need to know?

I don't need Carole's help. All I need is a fair court date, with a fair judge.

Everyone knows I was never a threat to Carole Baskin's physical safety. I was a threat to her monopolization of the big-cat trade; that is why I am in prison.

I at this time will *never* support the Big Cat Public Safety Act the way it is written because it only hurts private zoos and owners and makes a monopoly for the AZA and GFAS. If Carole wants to end the exploitation of tigers in America, let's end it all, not just some of it. Don't half-ass it just so Carole and the people she likes can continue to get rich. I will support a bill that gets tigers out of cages completely, including the cats at Big Cat Rescue and all their friends. Get me a deal and you will have my cooperation in shutting down the whole damn industry.

My case was never really about murder-for-hire. Carole Baskin going to the press about supporting my pardon shows me it was all a bullshit setup.

Howard Baskin says I could be a hero. Let me tell you who could be a hero: the person who comes forward and admits that federal agents and prosecutors conspired to put an innocent man in prison. Whoever comes forward with the real truth would be so famous and rich they would never have to work again.

Who wants to be a hero?

# ACKNOWLEDGMENTS

First and foremost I would like to thank my brother Garold Wayne Schreibvogel for teaching me that the most precious thing you have on this planet is your word.

Thank you to Brian Rhyne, my first husband, for all the years he put in cooking, cleaning, and doing the books at the pet store and believing in me enough to follow my dream to the zoo even as sick as he was.

My parents, Francis and Shirley Schreibvogel, for being my number one fans and for all the financial help they gave me to help make my dreams come true.

Ronnie Sands, for all the days and nights of sitting by my side at the hospital making sure I was going to pull through and for being there for the beatings I took from the abusive relationships.

Anne Patrick, for being there when all I wanted to do was die when Travis died.

Travis Michael Maldonado, who gave me part of my last name

I have today as I write this. He was my protector from everything and everyone.

To all of the people who I have lost: Deb Garton, Randy Lucas, Scotty from the Tiger Truck Stop, Wendy Templeton, Alisa Finley, Lana Shingles, and little Katie.

Shellie Hier, for sticking by me to help with my parents and to continue to fight to help me save my own life.

Kimber Finlay, my little angel sent from God to give me someone to spoil and be my little medium to talk to Travis for me.

Special thanks to the 225 tigers and lions that adopted me as one of their own; to Joe, Lilly, Bo, and Bongo, my chimps; to Luke, the bull elephant who taught me that everything has a soul; to all of the animals that God gifted me with the chance to come to know.

To God, the Lord, for getting me this far and for giving me the gift to walk among the greatest beasts.